ERIC LANLARD'S
Afternoon Tea

To Paul for his continuous support and encouragement

An Hachette UK Company www.hachette.co.uk

First published in Great Britain in 2016 by Mitchell Beazley,
a division of Octopus Publishing Group Ltd
Carmelite House, 50 Victoria Embankment, London EC4Y 0DZ
www.octopusbooks.co.uk

Distributed in the US by Hachette Book Group
1290 Avenue of the Americas, 4th and 5th Floors, New York, NY 10020
www.octopusbooksusa.com

Distributed in Canada by Canadian Manda Group
664 Annette St., Toronto, Ontario, Canada M6S 2C8

A CIP catalogue record for this book is available from the British Library.
Printed and bound in China

1 3 5 7 9 10 8 6 4 2

Publisher Alison Starling
Managing Editor Sybella Stephens
Copy Editor Jo Murray
Art Director Juliette Norsworthy
Designer Penny Stock
Photographer Kate Whitaker
Food Styling Eric Lanlard and Lizzie Kamenetzky
Prop Stylist Liz Belton
Recipe Tester Lizzie Kamenetzky
Production Controller Allison Gonsalves

Both imperial and metric measurements have been given in all recipes. Use one set
of measurements only and not a mixture of both.
Eggs should be medium and milk should be full fat unless otherwise stated.
This book includes dishes made with nuts and nut derivatives.

ERIC LANLARD'S

Afternoon Tea

ERIC LANLARD

MITCHELL
BEAZLEY

Contents

Introduction 6

Matching teas to food 8

How to make a perfect cup of tea 9

Afternoon tea menus 10

Macarons and choux 12

Savoury tarts 32

Sandwiches and scones 48

Cakes and sweet tarts 82

Pâtisserie 126

Biscuits 152

Index 172

Acknowledgements 176

Introduction

I experienced my first British afternoon tea at the tender age of seven when my Anglophile mother took me on an overnight ferry trip across the channel to England. She had read in a magazine it was the ultimate British tradition and wanted to experience it. After what felt like hours on a bus, we arrived at a proper tea room where we were served a traditional cream tea. We hadn't anticipated quite how much food would be served, and having just eaten lunch beforehand we were full very quickly. Before we embarked on our ferry home, my mum purchased a fine china floral tea service from one of the souvenir shops in Portsmouth – her idea was to replicate our experience back home for friends. However, it wasn't so easy – we soon discovered that clotted cream was only available in the UK, and none of mum's French baking books featured a recipe for scones. Despite this we made it happen and, of course, I was always the first to volunteer to help in the kitchen or set the table. How funny to think, all these years later, I am now an expert on the art of afternoon tea and I have designed and served my afternoon tea experiences on luxury cruise ships, at 5-star hotels all over the world and at Cake Boy, my pâtisserie in London.

Afternoon tea is a fun and very glamorous experience, usually served in beautiful surroundings, and a very relaxed way to meet friends or celebrate an occasion without being rushed. Some people might say that afternoon tea is the new lunch! Like most things, the afternoon tea has evolved and has become more interactive in recent years, involving enticing themes and featuring new ingredients or baking techniques.

The same goes for the tea; in recent years we have learned so much about tea and are now enjoying many more new flavours or blends that can be matched to food. Many top hotels now employ a tea sommelier who can guide you through the ceremony of choosing and brewing the perfect cup.

In this book, I wanted to share with you my passion for baking, but also my love for afternoon tea, and provide the ideas for you to create your own gorgeous afternoon tea at home. Whether you want to celebrate a special occasion or simply entertain friends and family, the following chapters include sweet and savoury recipes from casual and rustic dishes to more flamboyant showpieces to suit any theme or occasion. Of course, I've included some classics with my own added twist as well as a few more innovative recipes that are sure to become talking points when served – this is what afternoon tea is all about: great food, great company, beautiful surroundings and memorable conversations. I think my mum will love this book – I expect the (now vintage) floral tea service will come out and I shall receive a request for some clotted cream to be sent to France very soon…

I hope you will enjoy cooking from this book as much as I have enjoyed writing it.

Happy baking!

Eric x

Matching teas to food

Just as you would with wine, tea should be paired with the food you are serving. In the Far East, tea is often served throughout a meal and great care goes into choosing which tea to serve. There are no rules dictating what tea should be served with which foods, but some teas complement certain flavours better than others.

White tea has a light, soft and very subtle flavour which, if paired with any strong-flavoured foods, will lose its natural sweetness and it will be impossible to detect its delicate flavour. This tea should be served without milk, and is the ideal choice to serve at the beginning of your afternoon tea in anticipation of the arrival of any food, after which you can move on to a stronger-flavoured tea.

Herbal infusions are a popular choice and there are a huge variety of different flavours, from fruits and flower blossoms to herbs and spices. Some blends may be too overpowering to pair with certain foods, so choose subtle flavours that will enhance your food instead of overwhelming it.

Green tea is another very popular choice. It has a subtle flavour, making it the perfect companion to mild-flavoured foods such as seafood or chicken, and should be served without milk. A good green tea is the perfect choice to serve with my Spinach Focaccia with Salmon and Keta Tartare (see page 52) or Herby Lobster Rolls (see page 59).

Some fruit-flavoured green teas have a light sweet flavour that would be a suitable accompaniment to fruit and pastries such as my Linzer Torte (see page 122).

Black tea has a full and robust flavour, therefore the type of foods that complement this tea best should be similarly strong so that one flavour is not dominating the other.

Ceylon has a smooth and citrusy flavour and will perfectly enhance sweet desserts such as my Black-bottom Cheesecake Squares (see page 128). Darjeeling is the perfect pairing to a creamy pastry, such as a fruit mousse, syllabub or even an éclair; it's the rich tea flavour and the cream that work so well together, so Darjeeling is best kept for sweet treats.

Earthy teas, such as Kenyan tea, bring out the richness in savoury snacks such as the Blue Cheese Gougères (see page 29), but also complement sweet pastries such as the dainty Tartelettes aux Fruits (see page 118).

Smoky tea like Lapsang Souchong is the perfect pairing with a chocolate cake such as my Chocolate Ganache Hearts (see page 147) – two powerful flavours!

Do try experimenting by tasting lots of different teas to see what you like best, as there are so many teas and blends now available.

How to make a perfect cup of tea

It all starts with the water – your ingredients are secondary; it doesn't matter if you use a tea bag or loose leaf tea, a horrible taste like chlorine, iron or sulphur can damage the taste and aroma of your tea. Fill a kettle with cold mineral or filtered water – do not use pre-boiled or distilled water, as the more oxygen there is in the water, the better your tea will taste.

Bring fresh water to the boil. Immediately fill your empty cup or teapot and leave for 5 minutes to warm. Fine china is a great insulator of heat that will keep your tea hotter for longer. Empty the water from your cup or teapot and refill with very hot (but not boiling) water. If the water is boiling or too hot you could destroy some of the complex flavours from the tea leaves. If using a cup, leave some space for the milk (if liked).

If using a tea bag, leave it to infuse for 3–5 minutes depending on the type of tea and how strong you like it, then remove the tea bag using a spoon. There is always an argument about when to add the milk (if using), but it has been proven that tea will infuse more effectively in just hot water rather than a mix of milk and water.

If using loose leaf tea, add one teaspoon of tea per person to the tea pot, plus one extra (this is the same if using a infuser). Using a preheated spoon, swirl the leaves in the water and leave to infuse for:
1 minute for green tea (don't leave for more than 2 minutes, as green tea will become bitter)
3 minutes for black tea
8–10 minutes for herbal or fruit infusions

The taste and flavours of loose tea leaves is incomparable to tea bags, even expensive brands. In the Far East the traditional way to use loose tea leaves is to add them first to very hot water to remove any impurities, and then infuse them in slightly cooler freshly drawn hot water.

Add sugar or honey to sweeten your tea, and what we call in France *un nuage de lait* (a cloud of milk) if you want, too. Sit back, relax and savour the moment with your perfect cup of tea.

Afternoon tea menus

Sweet valentine

Parma ham and fig macarons
(see page 21)

Raw cacao and raspberry scones
(see page 74)

Lemon posset (see page 137)

Chocolate ganache hearts (see page 147)

Serve with Earl Grey tea

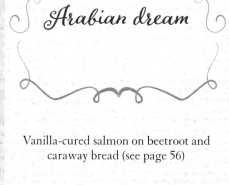

Arabian dream

Vanilla-cured salmon on beetroot and
caraway bread (see page 56)

Pistachio and rose scones (see page 73)

Clementine and pomegranate cake
(see page 103)

Persian syllabub (see page 140)

*Serve with a rich vanilla-flavoured
black tea*

Mother's day

Brie and red onion marmalade Gruyère
éclairs (see page 24)

Classic buttermilk scones (see page 68)

Light Italian fruit cake (see page 104)

Strawberry ombré cake (see page 112)

*Serve with a sweet and fruity red berry
herbal tea or hibiscus infusion*

Al fresco summer picnic

Lemon and pepper macarons with smoked salmon (see page 14)

Aperol sultana scones (see page 78)

Matcha and lemon cake (see page 116)

Lavender shortbread hearts (see page 163)

Serve with a zesty and fresh Lady Grey black tea

Autumn comfort

Hazelnut macarons with pumpkin purée (see page 16)

Cheese scones (see page 81)

Scandinavian apple cake (see page 94)

Peruvian chocolate and orange mousse (see page 134)

Serve with a rich and smoky Lapsang Souchong black tea

Celebration

Tequila king prawn sliders (see page 60)

Orange blossom and bee pollen scones (see page 69)

Fresh fig cake (see page 106)

Red velvet cheesecake (see page 130)

Serve with a fine floral or fruity green tea

Macarons and choux

Lemon and pepper macarons with smoked salmon

This is a great combination; the lemony, peppery macarons still taste sweet, which complements the smokiness of the salmon. The addition of grapefruit gives some extra zing without being overpowering… your taste buds will be confused!

100g (3½oz) ground almonds
100g (3½oz) icing sugar
90g (3¼oz) egg whites (about 3 eggs)
100g (3½oz) golden caster sugar
1 tsp freshly cracked black pepper, plus extra for sprinkling
1 tsp lemon extract
a few drops of yellow food colouring

For the filling
280g (10oz) cream cheese
300g (10½oz) smoked salmon, sliced
18–20 small white grapefruit segments
dill sprigs

Line 2 baking sheets with baking paper. Put the ground almonds and icing sugar into a food processor and whizz until finely ground, then sift into a bowl to make a fine powder. Set aside.

In a large, clean, dry bowl, whisk the egg whites to soft peaks, then add the caster sugar a little at a time, whisking until the mixture is stiff and glossy. Using a rubber spatula, gradually fold the almond powder, black pepper, lemon extract and food colouring into the egg whites until the mixture is smooth and shiny and just falls in a ribbon from your spatula.

Spoon the mixture into a piping bag fitted with a 1cm (½in) diameter plain piping nozzle, then pipe discs about 4cm (1½in) in diameter on to the prepared baking sheets. Sprinkle a little extra black pepper over each macaron. Give the base of each baking sheet a sharp tap against the work surface to ensure a good 'foot', then leave to stand for 10–30 minutes at room temperature to allow the tops to dry out. (You should be able to gently touch the surface of a macaron without it sticking to your finger.) Meanwhile, preheat the oven to 150°C (fan 130°C)/300°F/gas mark 2.

Bake in the oven for 12–15 minutes, or until the baking paper peels off easily from the macarons, briefly opening the door after 10 minutes to let out the steam. Leave to cool on the baking sheets until almost cold, then transfer to a cooling rack to cool completely.

To make the filling, put the cream cheese into a bowl and beat until soft, then spoon into a piping bag and pipe a little on to the base of a macaron. Top with a slice of smoked salmon, a grapefruit segment and a frond of dill. Pipe a little more cream cheese on to the base of a second macaron, then secure at an angle on top of the filling. Repeat with the remaining macarons and store in an airtight container in the refrigerator for up to 24 hours until ready to serve.

Hazelnut macarons with pumpkin purée

The flavours of this macaron shout autumn! I simply love the smell in my kitchen when these are baking slowly in the oven. The addition of the salty chicken crackling and succulent pumpkin filling really brings together that home-cooked comfort food flavour.

225g (8oz) icing sugar
115g (4oz) hazelnuts, roasted and chopped (see Tip on page 17)
generous pinch of salt
140g (5oz) egg whites
70g (2½oz) caster sugar

a few drops of orange food colouring
chicken crackling (see Tip), for dusting

For the filling
400g (14oz) canned pumpkin purée
100g (3½oz) ground hazelnuts
5 tbsp double cream
½ tsp mixed spice
salt and freshly ground black pepper

Line 2 baking sheets with baking paper. Put the icing sugar, chopped hazelnuts and salt into a food processor and whizz until finely ground, then sift into a bowl to make a fine powder. Set aside.

In a large, clean, dry bowl, whisk the egg whites to soft peaks, then add the caster sugar a little at a time, whisking until the mixture is stiff and glossy. Using a rubber spatula, fold the hazelnut powder and food colouring into the egg whites until the mixture is smooth and shiny and just falls in a ribbon from your spatula.

Spoon the mixture into a piping bag fitted with a 1cm (½in) diameter plain piping nozzle, then pipe discs about 4cm (1½in) in diameter on to the prepared baking sheets. Dust a little of the chicken crackling over each macaron. Give the base of each baking sheet a sharp tap against the work surface to ensure a good 'foot', then leave to stand for 10–30 minutes at room temperature to allow the tops to dry out. (You should be able to gently touch the surface of a macaron without it sticking to your finger.)

Meanwhile, preheat the oven to 150°C (fan 130°C)/300°F/gas mark 2.

Bake in the oven for 12–15 minutes, or until the baking paper peels off easily from the macarons, briefly opening the door after 10 minutes to let out the steam. Leave to cool on the baking sheets until almost cold, then transfer to a cooling rack to cool completely.

To make the filling, press the pumpkin through a muslin cloth into a bowl to remove any excess water (the drier the pumpkin the better). Mix in the ground hazelnuts, cream and mixed spice and season well. Spoon into a piping bag and pipe a little on to the base of a macaron. Sandwich together with a second macaron. Repeat with the remaining macarons, then store in an airtight container in the refrigerator for up to 24 hours until ready to serve.

Tip ~ To make chicken crackling, remove the skin from 2 chicken breasts. Lay it flat between 2 roasting trays and roast in a preheated oven, 200°C (fan 180°C)/400°F/gas mark 6, for 10–15 minutes until really crisp. Cool, then crumble.

Walnut and dolcelatte macarons

The secret to perfecting a savoury macaron is to get the balance right between the natural sweetness and the salty ingredients, and this is the perfect match: creamy Italian blue cheese and nutty roasted walnuts. The sweet macaron shells bring a delicate smoothness to this incredible flavour combination.

50g (1¾oz) ground almonds

50g (1¾oz) walnuts, roasted and finely ground (see Tip)

100g (3½oz) icing sugar

90g (3¼oz) egg whites (about 3 eggs)

100g (3½oz) golden caster sugar

1 tsp freshly cracked black pepper, plus extra for sprinkling

For the filling

250g (9oz) dolcelatte cheese

50g (1¾oz) walnuts, roasted and crushed

Line 2 baking sheets with baking paper. Put the ground almonds, ground walnuts and icing sugar into a food processor and whizz until finely ground, then sift into a bowl to make a fine powder. Set aside.

In a large, clean, dry bowl, whisk the egg whites to soft peaks, then add the caster sugar a little at a time, whisking until the mixture is stiff and glossy. Using a rubber spatula, gradually fold the nut powder and black pepper into the egg whites until the mixture is smooth and shiny and just falls in a ribbon from your spatula.

Spoon the mixture into a piping bag fitted with a 1cm (½in) diameter plain piping nozzle, then pipe discs about 4cm (1½in) in diameter on to the prepared baking sheets. Sprinkle a little extra black pepper over each macaron. Give the base of each baking sheet a sharp tap against the work surface to ensure a good 'foot', then leave to stand for 10–30 minutes at room temperature to allow the tops to dry out. (You should be able to gently touch the surface of a macaron without it sticking to your finger.) Meanwhile, preheat the oven to 150°C (fan 130°C)/300°F/gas mark 2.

Bake in the oven for 12–15 minutes, or until the baking paper peels off easily from the macarons, briefly opening the door after 10 minutes to let out the steam. Leave to cool on the baking sheets until almost cold, then transfer to a cooling rack to cool completely.

To make the filling, place the cheese in a small bowl and beat until smooth, then fold in the crushed walnuts. Spread a little of the mixture on to the base of a macaron, then sandwich together with a second macaron. Repeat with the remaining macarons, then store in an airtight container in the refrigerator for up to 24 hours until ready to serve.

Tip ~ For roasted walnuts or any other nuts, simply spread whole nuts over a baking tray and roast in the oven at 180°C (fan 160°C)/350°F/gas mark 4 for 8–10 minutes, or until golden and crisp – be sure to watch them, as they can burn quickly. Leave to cool, then chop or grind in a food processor as the recipe requires.

LEFT Beetroot and coriander macarons
RIGHT Parma ham and fig macarons

Beetroot and coriander macarons

These pretty macarons will provide a glorious injection of colour to any afternoon tea. With a delicate combination of flavours, the zesty filling balances the sweetness of the shells.

50g (1¾oz) ground almonds
50g (1¾oz) walnuts, roasted and finely ground (see Tip on page 17)
100g (3½oz) icing sugar
90g (3¼oz) egg whites (about 3 eggs)
100g (3½oz) golden caster sugar
a few drops of red food colouring
1 tbsp poppy seeds, for sprinkling

For the filling
250g (9oz) cooked beetroot
50g (1¾oz) thick Greek yogurt
¼ tsp ground coriander
¼ tsp ground cumin
squeeze of lemon juice, to taste
micro coriander leaves
salt and freshly ground black pepper

Line 2 baking sheets with baking paper. Put the ground almonds, ground walnuts and icing sugar into a food processor and whizz until finely ground, then sift into a bowl to make a fine powder. Set aside.

In a large, clean, dry bowl, whisk the egg whites to soft peaks, then add the caster sugar a little at a time, whisking until the mixture is stiff and glossy. Using a rubber spatula, gradually fold the nut powder and food colouring into the egg whites until the mixture is smooth and shiny and just falls in a ribbon from your spatula.

Spoon the mixture into a piping bag fitted with a 1cm (½in) diameter plain piping nozzle, then pipe discs about 4cm (1½in) in diameter on to the prepared baking sheets. Sprinkle poppy seeds over each macaron. Give the base of each baking sheet a sharp tap against the work surface to ensure a good 'foot', then leave to stand for 10–30 minutes at room temperature to allow

the tops to dry out. (You should be able to gently touch the surface of a macaron without it sticking to your finger.) Meanwhile, preheat the oven to 150°C (fan 130°C)/300°F/gas mark 2.

Bake in the oven for 12–15 minutes, or until the baking paper peels off easily from the macarons, briefly opening the door after 10 minutes to let out the steam. Leave to cool on the baking sheets until almost cold, then transfer to a cooling rack to cool completely.

To make the filling, place all the ingredients except the coriander leaves in a food processor and whizz until creamy and smooth, then season and spoon into a piping bag. Pipe a little on to the base of a macaron and top with a few coriander leaves. Secure a second macaron at an angle on top of the filling. Repeat with the remaining macarons, then store in an airtight container in the refrigerator for up to 24 hours until ready to serve.

Makes 18–20 | **Preparation time:** 30 minutes, plus standing and cooling | **Cooking time:** 12–15 minutes

Parma ham and fig macarons

I could eat plenty of these macarons! I love the colour and the nigella seed topping which looks very striking. Both the macaron shells and the Parma ham bring a lovely sweetness that complement the fresh figs. If figs are out of season try substituting pieces of cantaloupe melon.

100g (3½oz) ground almonds
100g (3½oz) icing sugar
90g (3¼oz) egg whites (about 3 eggs)
100g (3½oz) golden caster sugar
a few drops of purple food colouring
1 tbsp nigella seeds, for sprinkling

For the filling
200g (7oz) mascarpone cheese
200g (7oz) thinly sliced Parma ham
8 ripe figs, each cut into 6 wedges
18–20 basil tips
salt and freshly ground black pepper

Line 2 baking sheets with baking paper. Put the ground almonds and icing sugar into a food processor and whizz until finely ground, then sift into a bowl to make a fine powder. Set aside.

In a large, clean, dry bowl, whisk the egg whites to soft peaks, then add the caster sugar a little at a time, whisking until the mixture is stiff and glossy. Using a rubber spatula, gradually fold the almond powder and food colouring into the egg whites until the mixture is smooth and shiny and just falls in a ribbon from your spatula.

Spoon the mixture into a piping bag fitted with a 1cm (½in) diameter plain piping nozzle, then pipe discs about 4cm (1½in) in diameter on to the prepared baking sheets. Sprinkle a few of the nigella seeds over each macaron. Give the base of each baking sheet a sharp tap against the work surface to ensure a good 'foot', then leave to stand for 10–30 minutes at room temperature to allow the tops to dry out.

(You should be able to gently touch the surface of a macaron without it sticking to your finger.) Meanwhile, preheat the oven to 150°C (fan 130°C)/300°F/gas mark 2.

Bake in the oven for 12–15 minutes, or until the baking paper peels off easily from the macarons, briefly opening the door after 10 minutes to let out the steam. Leave to cool on the baking sheets until almost cold, then transfer to a cooling rack to cool completely.

To make the filling, put the mascarpone in a bowl and beat until smooth, then season well. Spoon into a piping bag and pipe a little on to the base of a macaron. Top with a lovely slice of Parma ham, a wedge of fig and a basil tip. Pipe a little more mascarpone on to the base of a second macaron, then secure at an angle on top of the filling. Repeat with the remaining macarons, then store in an airtight container in the refrigerator for up to 24 hours until ready to serve.

LEFT Porcini and pancetta éclairs
RIGHT Brie and red onion
marmalade Gruyère éclairs

Porcini and pancetta éclairs

Another great savoury éclair, this time with added crushed walnuts sprinkled over just before baking for a great delicious crunch. The filling is rich and sweet from the addition of the pancetta and maple syrup… a great winter offering.

2 tsp porcini powder (see Tip)

1 x quantity Classic Choux Pastry (see page 36)

beaten egg, to glaze

1 tbsp finely crushed walnuts

For the filling

6 smoked pancetta slices

3 tbsp maple syrup

60g (2¼oz) unsalted butter

2 spring onions, finely chopped

1 tsp dried chilli flakes

60g (2¼oz) plain flour

200ml (7fl oz) milk

40g (1½oz) mature Cheddar cheese, grated

2 tsp porcini powder (see Tip)

freshly ground black pepper

Preheat the oven to 200°C (fan 180°C)/400°F/gas mark 6. Line 2 baking sheets with baking paper.

Fold the porcini powder into the choux paste, then tip into a piping bag fitted with a 1cm (½in) diameter plain piping nozzle. Pipe éclairs, about 8cm (3¼in) long, on to the prepared sheets. Brush with beaten egg and sprinkle over the walnuts. Bake in the oven for 20–25 minutes until puffed up and golden.

Remove the éclairs from the oven (leave the oven on) and pierce the bases with a sharp knife to release the steam, then transfer to a cooling rack to cool.

Meanwhile, make the filling. Lay the pancetta on a baking sheet and drizzle with maple syrup. Bake in the hot oven for about 10 minutes or until golden and crispy. Set aside.

In a medium saucepan, heat the butter until melted, add the spring onions and chilli flakes and cook for 1 minute, then add the flour and cook for 2 minutes, stirring with a wooden spoon. Add the milk a little at the time, stirring continuously with a balloon whisk to prevent lumps forming. When thickened and smooth, add the cheese and cook until melted, stirring continuously, then add the porcini powder and season with black pepper.

Crumble the crispy pancetta into tiny pieces, then fold into the porcini sauce. Cover with clingfilm and leave to cool.

Spoon the cheese and bacon sauce into a piping bag fitted with a 1cm (½in) diameter plain piping nozzle. Slice the cooled éclairs horizontally using a sharp serrated knife, then pipe in the sauce and top with the lids. Chill in the refrigerator for up to 24 hours until ready to serve.

Tip~ To make porcini powder, put dried porcini mushrooms in a mini chopper or blender and whizz until they form a fine powder.

Brie and red onion marmalade Gruyère éclairs

Savoury choux pastry is a treat, but you don't always have to make profiteroles. With a golden cheese gratinée topping and a gorgeous filling of slow-cooked onion marmalade, creamy Brie and peppery rocket, these éclairs are perfect for an afternoon tea.

1 x quantity Classic Choux Pastry (see page 36)

beaten egg, to glaze

85g (3oz) Gruyère cheese, grated

For the filling

400g (14oz) soft Brie cheese, thinly sliced

large handful of rocket leaves

1 bunch of basil

2 tsp extra virgin olive oil

For the red onion marmalade

5 red onions, finely sliced

good knob of unsalted butter

2 tsp water

salt and freshly ground black pepper

Preheat the oven to 200°C (fan 180°C)/400°F/gas mark 6. Line 2 baking sheets with baking paper.

Tip the choux pastry into a piping bag fitted with a 1cm (½in) diameter plain piping nozzle. Pipe mini éclairs, about 8cm (3¼in) long, on to the prepared baking sheets. Brush with beaten egg and sprinkle generously with the Gruyère. Bake in the oven for 20–25 minutes until puffed up and golden.

Meanwhile, make the red onion marmalade. Put the onions, butter and the 2 teaspoons water into a medium heavy-based saucepan, cover with a lid and cook over a low heat for at least 10 minutes until the onions are very soft. Remove the lid and continue to cook, stirring, for 10–12 minutes or until the onions are caramelized. Season and leave to cool.

Remove the éclairs from the oven and pierce the bases with a sharp knife to release the steam, then transfer to a cooling rack to cool completely.

Slice the cooled éclairs horizontally using a sharp serrated knife. Spoon a good layer of the cold marmalade into each éclair base, then top with a couple of Brie slices. In a bowl, toss together the rocket, basil leaves and olive oil. Arrange a little of the salad on the Brie, then top with the éclair lids at an angle. Chill in the refrigerator for up to 24 hours until ready to serve.

Tip ~ Before piping out the choux pastry, first use a little of the paste to secure the baking paper to each corner of the baking sheets.

LEFT Blue cheese gougères
RIGHT Caprice profiteroles

Makes 25–30 | Preparation time: 30 minutes, plus cooling | Cooking time: 25–30 minutes

Blue cheese gougères

Gougères are a French pâtisserie classic; these little mouthfuls are filled to bursting with a moreish blue cheese béchamel sauce – sure to be a hit with all cheese lovers. You can substitute Cheddar cheese for the blue cheese if you prefer.

For the pastry
150ml (¼ pint) water
60g (2¼oz) unsalted butter, cut into small cubes
generous pinch of salt
100g (3½oz) plain flour, sifted
2 large eggs, beaten
85g (3oz) Gruyère cheese, grated
beaten egg, to glaze

For the filling
50g (1¾oz) unsalted butter
40g (1½oz) plain flour
250ml (9fl oz) milk
50g (1¾oz) blue cheese
freshly grated nutmeg
freshly ground black pepper

Preheat the oven to 200°C (fan 180°C)/400°F/gas mark 6. Line 2 baking sheets with baking paper.

Put the 150ml (¼ pint) water, the butter and salt into a medium saucepan and heat gently until the butter is melted, then bring to the boil. Immediately remove the pan from the heat and tip in all the flour. Beat with a wooden spoon until the ingredients bind together to form a dough. Return the pan to a medium heat and continue to beat until the dough comes away from the sides of the pan and forms a smooth ball in the centre. Leave to cool for 2–3 minutes, then gradually beat in the eggs to form a smooth, shiny paste. Stir in three-quarters of the Gruyère.

Tip the paste into a piping bag fitted with a 1cm (½in) diameter plain piping nozzle and pipe profiterole-sized balls on to the prepared baking sheets. Brush with beaten egg and sprinkle over the remaining Gruyère. Bake in the oven for 20–25 minutes until puffed up and beautifully golden.

Meanwhile, make the filling. In a small saucepan, heat the butter until melted, add the flour and cook for 2 minutes, stirring with a wooden spoon. Add the milk a little at the time, stirring continuously with a balloon whisk to prevent lumps forming. When thickened and smooth, crumble in the blue cheese and heat until melted, stirring continuously. Add a good grating of nutmeg and season with pepper. Cover with clingfilm and leave to cool.

Remove the gougères from the oven and pierce the bases with a sharp knife to release the steam, then transfer to a cooling rack to cool.

Spoon the cheese mixture into a piping bag fitted with a 5mm (¼in) diameter plain piping nozzle. Pipe a generous amount into each cooled gougère through the small hole you made with the knife. Chill in the refrigerator until ready to serve.

Caprice profiteroles

These are like little bite-sized rays of sunshine! Crispy on the outside and fluffy on the inside and filled with what always reminds me of an Italian summer.

1 x quantity Classic Choux Pastry (see page 36)

beaten egg, to glaze

2 tsp poppy seeds

2 tsp olive oil

12 plum cherry tomatoes, sliced

2 garlic cloves, crushed

handful of basil leaves, chopped

12 mini mozzarella balls, halved

freshly ground black pepper

Preheat the oven to 200°C (fan 180°C)/400°F/gas mark 6.
Line 2 baking sheets with baking paper.

Tip the choux pastry into a piping bag fitted with a 1cm (½in) diameter plain piping nozzle. Pipe profiteroles on to the prepared baking sheets, then brush with the beaten egg and sprinkle with the poppy seeds. Bake in the oven for 20–25 minutes until puffed up and golden. Pierce the bases with a sharp knife to release the steam, then transfer to a cooling rack to cool.

Slice the tops off the cooled profiteroles and place the bases on a baking sheet. Bake for 5 minutes in a preheated oven, 180°C (fan 160°C)/350°F/gas mark 4, to dry them out, then leave to cool completely.

Meanwhile, heat the olive oil in a small frying pan, add the tomatoes and garlic and cook for a couple of minutes until the tomatoes are slightly softened but still retain some firmness. Season with pepper. Remove from the heat and stir in the basil, then leave to cool.

Place half a mozzarella ball on the base of each profiterole, then spoon over a slice of tomato and some of the basil. Top with the profiterole lids and serve.

Mini salmon mousse and nigella seed Paris-Brest

This is my savoury take on the French pâtisserie classic. The filling is a smooth smoked salmon mousse with a luxurious addition of salmon roe which sparkles under the crispy lid of the Paris-Brest.

1 x quantity Classic Choux Pastry (see page 36)

beaten egg, to glaze

2 tsp nigella seeds

100g (3½oz) smoked salmon

250g (9oz) ricotta cheese

3 tbsp double cream

juice of ½ lemon

3 tsp chopped dill, plus extra to garnish

50g (1¾oz) keta (salmon roe)

freshly ground black pepper

Preheat the oven to 200°C (fan 180°C)/400°F/gas mark 6.
Line 2 baking sheets with baking paper.

Tip the choux pastry into a piping bag fitted with a 1cm (½in) diameter star-shaped piping nozzle. Pipe 5cm (2in) diameter mini Paris-Brest (rings) on to the prepared baking sheets. Brush with the beaten egg and sprinkle over the nigella seeds. Bake in the oven for 20–25 minutes until puffed up and golden. Pierce the side of each with a sharp knife to let the steam escape, then transfer to a cooling rack to cool completely.

Meanwhile, make the salmon mousse. Place the smoked salmon, ricotta, cream, lemon juice and black pepper in a food processor and blitz until smooth, then fold in the dill. Spoon the mixture into a piping bag fitted with a 5mm (¼in) diameter star-shaped piping nozzle and leave to set in the refrigerator.

Slice the tops off the cooled Paris-Brest, then pipe small rosettes of the salmon mousse into the bases and add a few salmon eggs. Garnish each Paris-Brest with dill, top with the lids and serve.

Savoury tarts

Tartelettes de Saint Jacques

Originating from Brittany, I had to include a regional recipe and this is one that brings back many childhood memories for me. Succulent scallops sitting on a delicious bed of cooked leek and tarragon are typical of Breton cooking – simple, and all about the delicious ingredients.

1 tbsp olive oil, plus extra for drizzling

30g (1oz) unsalted butter, plus extra for greasing

3 leeks, white part only, trimmed, cleaned and thinly sliced

4 tbsp crème fraîche

1 large egg, beaten

1 tbsp finely chopped tarragon

1 x quantity chilled Shortcrust Pastry (see page 36)

plain flour, for dusting

6 king scallops (or 12 queenies)

salt and freshly ground black pepper

chervil sprigs, for garnishing

Preheat the oven to 180°C (fan 160°C)/350°F/gas mark 4.
Heat the oil and half the butter in a frying pan, add the leeks and cook for 5 minutes until they are soft and glossy. Tip into a bowl, stir in the crème fraîche, egg and tarragon and season well. Set aside.

Grease 12 x individual 5cm (2in) diameter tartlet tins or a 12-hole patty tin. Roll out the pastry on a lightly floured surface as thinly as you can. Using a 6cm (2½in) diameter fluted cookie cutter, stamp out 12 discs, re-rolling the trimmings as necessary, and use to line the tins, then chill in the refrigerator for 15 minutes. Divide the leek mixture among the pastry cases and bake in the oven for 15 minutes until golden and set.

Meanwhile, heat the remaining butter in a heavy-based nonstick frying pan and cook the scallops until golden on both sides and just cooked through, making sure not to overcook them. Season the scallops and cut in half horizontally (unless using queenies).

Place a scallop half on top of each hot tart, drizzle with a little olive oil and garnish with chervil. Serve immediately.

Classic choux pastry

55g (2oz) unsalted butter, cut into small cubes
generous pinch of salt
150ml (¼ pint) water
75g (2½oz) plain flour, sifted
2 eggs, beaten

Put the butter, salt and the 150ml (¼ pint) water into a saucepan and heat gently until the butter is melted, then bring to the boil.

Immediately remove the pan from the heat and quickly tip in all the flour. Beat with a wooden spoon until the ingredients bind together to form a dough.

Return the pan to a medium heat and continue to beat until the dough comes away from the sides of the pan and forms a smooth ball in the centre.

Leave to cool for 2–3 minutes, then gradually beat in the eggs to form a smooth, shiny paste. Beat vigorously.

Use the choux paste immediately, following the recipe instructions.

Shortcrust pastry

125g (4½oz) plain flour
75g (2½oz) cold unsalted butter, diced
pinch of salt
1 egg yolk

Put the flour into a bowl, add the butter and rub in using your fingertips until it resembles the texture of sand. Add the salt and egg yolk and mix together to form a dough, adding a few drops of cold water if the mixture is too dry. Knead briefly, being careful not to overwork it. Shape into a disc, cover with clingfilm and chill in the refrigerator for 30 minutes.

Pear, Roquefort and walnut tartlets

I love eating blue cheese with pears; the addition of the pear adds an extra touch of sweetness to this little tartlet. Of course, you can use any blue cheese you like.

unsalted butter, for greasing

375g (13oz) ready-made all-butter puff pastry

plain flour, for dusting

150g (5½oz) Roquefort cheese (or any blue cheese)

4–5 tbsp double cream

1 tsp paprika, plus extra for dusting

a few thyme sprigs, leaves stripped

2 ripe pears, peeled, cored and diced

1 tbsp roasted and chopped walnuts (see Tip on page 17), plus 24 walnut halves

salt and freshly ground black pepper

Preheat the oven to 200°C (fan 180°C)/400°F/gas mark 6.

Grease 24 x individual 5cm (2in) diameter tartlet tins or 2 x 12-hole mini tart tins. Roll out the pastry on a lightly floured surface to 2mm (¹⁄₁₆in) thick. Using a 6cm (2½in) diameter plain cookie cutter, stamp out 24 discs and use to line the tins. Place on a baking sheet (if using individual tins) and chill in the refrigerator for 30 minutes.

In a small bowl, crumble the cheese, then gradually add the cream until the mixture is smooth and without any lumps. Add the paprika and thyme leaves, then season well. Fold in the pears and chopped walnuts.

Divide the mixture between the tart cases and dust generously with a little more paprika. Top each with a walnut half and bake in the oven for 20 minutes until golden and set. Serve warm.

LEFT Curried crab filo tartlets
MIDDLE Tartes flambées
RIGHT Pear, Roquefort and
walnut tartlets

Curried crab filo tartlets

I tried my first spicy crab tart when visiting Singapore and I thought it would make a great addition to an afternoon tea. The spicing is subtle and complements the sweet crab meat. I love using filo pastry for this delicate recipe.

50g (1¾oz) unsalted butter, melted, plus extra for greasing
5 sheets of filo pastry, each about 24 x 45cm (9½ x 18in)
5 tbsp Greek yogurt
4 tbsp single cream
1 tsp curry powder
¼ tsp mustard powder
2 eggs
2 tsp chopped fresh coriander
1 red chilli, finely chopped
200g (7oz) white crab meat
salt and freshly ground black pepper
fresh thyme, to garnish

Preheat the oven to 200°C (fan 180°C)/400°F/gas mark 6. Grease a 12-hole muffin tin or 2 x 12-hole mini muffin tins with some of the melted butter.

Lay the filo sheets on a work surface, one on top of the other. Cut the stack into 12 squares (or if using mini muffin tins, cut into 9cm (3½in) squares). Brush a square of filo with melted butter, then top with a second square, offset to the first, and brush with more butter. Top with a third square and brush with butter again, then press into a mini muffin hole. Repeat with the remaining pastry to fill both trays.

Bake in the oven for 3–4 minutes until lightly golden, then leave to cool in the trays. Reduce the oven temperature to 180°C (fan 160°C)/350°F/gas mark 4.

Put the yogurt, cream, curry powder, mustard powder, a pinch of salt, a pinch of pepper and the eggs into a food processor and blitz until smooth and creamy, then fold in the coriander and chilli.

Fill the tart cases with the crab meat, then pour over the creamy filling, waiting for it to trickle through the crab meat and topping up if necessary. Bake for a further 12–15 minutes, or until golden and set. Garnish with thyme and serve warm.

Tartes flambées

This is a mini version of the traditional Alsace French tart. Heart-warming and packed with rich flavours, these little tarts always bring back memories of winter holidays in France, where they are served on the way back from a day skiing in the mountains.

unsalted butter, for greasing
1 x quantity chilled Shortcrust Pastry (see page 36)
plain flour, for dusting
olive oil, for frying
100g (3½oz) smoked lardons
½ white onion, finely chopped
100g (3½oz) thick crème fraîche
a few thyme sprigs, leaves stripped
freshly ground black pepper

Preheat the oven to 180°C (fan 160°C)/350°F/gas mark 4. Grease a 12-hole mini tart tin or 12 x individual 5cm (2in) diameter tartlet tins with the butter.

Roll out the pastry on a lightly floured surface to 3mm (⅛in) thick. Using a 6cm (2½in) diameter plain cookie cutter, stamp out 12 discs and use to line either your individual tins or your 12-hole mini tart tin. Place on a baking sheet (if using individual tins) and chill in the refrigerator for 30 minutes.

Heat up a little oil in a frying pan, add the lardons and cook until golden. Add the onion and cook, stirring a couple of times, then remove from the heat.

Put the crème fraîche into a bowl and season with pepper, then spoon into the tart cases, filling them one-third full. Top with the lardon mixture and sprinkle over some thyme leaves.

Bake in the oven for 10–12 minutes until golden. Leave to cool in the tins for a few minutes, then remove and serve warm.

Mini tomato, olive and mozzarella tarts

Sometimes the simplest combinations are the best, and this is true for these colourful tomato, olive and mozzarella tarts. Partially cooking the heirloom tomatoes brings out their flavour and texture.

unsalted butter, for greasing

olive oil, for frying

15–20 red and yellow cherry tomatoes, halved

1 garlic clove, thinly sliced

15 black olives, pitted and chopped

24 basil leaves

1 x quantity chilled Shortcrust Pastry (see page 36)

plain flour, for dusting

6 mini mozzarella balls, halved

salt and freshly ground black pepper

Preheat the oven to 180°C (fan 160°C)/350°F/gas mark 4. Heat a little olive oil in a large frying pan, add the tomatoes and garlic and sauté for 4–5 minutes until the tomatoes are tender but not overcooked. Add the olives and season, then tip into a bowl and leave to cool.

Heat a good layer of olive oil in the pan and fry the basil leaves for a few seconds until crisp and translucent, taking care as they will spit and splutter. Remove and drain on kitchen paper.

Roll out the pastry on a lightly floured surface to 2mm (1/16in) thick. Using a 7cm (2¾in) diameter plain cookie cutter, stamp out 12 discs, re-rolling the trimmings as necessary. Grease 12 x individual 6cm (2½in) diameter tartlet tins or a 12-hole mini tart tin, line with the pastry discs and prick with a fork. Bake in the oven for 6–8 minutes until golden. Leave to cool in the tins for 5 minutes, then transfer to a cooling rack to cool completely.

Fill the mini tart cases with the tomato and olive mixture, then top each with a mozzarella half and garnish with 2 crispy basil leaves. Serve immediately.

Camembert and apple tarts with a walnut drizzle

For me, this tart is pure comfort food: pan-fried apples covered with oozing Camembert cheese and fragrant walnut oil on top of a buttery, crispy puff pastry base – perfect for an autumn or winter afternoon tea.

25g (1oz) unsalted butter
2 firm dessert apples such as Granny Smith or Cox, peeled and cut into thin wedges
1 tbsp clear honey
2 tbsp balsamic vinegar

375g (13oz) ready-made all-butter puff pastry
plain flour, for dusting
150g (5½oz) Camembert, sliced

For the walnut drizzle
50g (1¾oz) walnuts
3–4 tbsp olive oil
1 tbsp chopped tarragon
salt and freshly ground black pepper

Preheat the oven to 200°C (fan 180°C)/400°F/gas mark 6.

Heat the butter in a pan, add the apples and fry until golden all over. Just before you remove the pan from the heat, stir in the honey and balsamic vinegar. Leave to cool.

Roll out the pastry on a lightly floured surface to 2mm (⅟₁₆in) thick. Using a 6cm (2½in) diameter plain cookie cutter, stamp out 12 discs. Grease 6 boat-shaped mini tart tins, about 12 x 5cm (4½ x 2in), and use 6 of the pastry discs to line the tins, trimming off any excess pastry. Place an empty tart tin on top of each lined tin and fill with baking beans or rice to prevent the pastry from puffing up.

Bake in the oven for 10 minutes, then remove the extra tart tins and beans. Return to the oven and bake for a further 2–3 minutes until cooked through and golden. Transfer the tart cases to a cooling rack. Leave the tart tins to cool, then repeat with the remaining pastry discs.

Meanwhile, make the walnut drizzle. Put the walnuts, oil, tarragon and salt and pepper into a food processor and blitz until it has the texture of pesto without being completely smooth. Set aside.

Fill the tart cases with the apple mixture and top each with a slice of Camembert. Bake in the oven for about 8 minutes until the cheese is all lovely and melted. Drizzle the walnut oil over the tarts to garnish. Serve warm.

Spinach and pine nut wholemeal tartlets

I had the idea to make these tarts from a Greek spinach pie that I love making at home in summer – these are a mini version, just without the pastry top, and make a perfect vegetarian option for your afternoon tea.

unsalted butter, for greasing

2 x quantities chilled Shortcrust Pastry (see page 36), made with 50:50 wholemeal flour and plain flour

plain flour, for dusting

300g (10½oz) frozen spinach, thawed and squeezed dry

150g (5½oz) ricotta cheese

2 tbsp grated Parmesan cheese

2 eggs, plus 1 egg yolk

freshly grated nutmeg

100g (3½oz) toasted pine nuts

salt and freshly ground black pepper

extra virgin olive oil, for drizzling

Grease 24 x individual 5cm (2in) diameter tartlet tins or 2 x 12-hole mini tart tins. Roll out the pastry on a floured surface as thinly as possible, making sure not to stretch it. Using a 6cm (2½in) diameter plain cookie cutter, stamp out 24 discs, re-rolling the trimmings as necessary. Use the pastry discs to line the prepared tins, then chill in the refrigerator for 15 minutes. Meanwhile, preheat the oven to 200°C (fan 180°C)/ 400°F/gas mark 6.

Put the spinach, ricotta, Parmesan, eggs and egg yolk and a good grating of nutmeg into a food processor or blender and blend until smooth. Season to taste, then stir in the pine nuts.

Divide the mixture among the tart cases and bake in the oven for 20 minutes until golden and set. Drizzle with a little extra virgin olive oil and serve warm.

Sandwiches and scones

LEFT Spinach focaccia with
salmon and keta tartare
RIGHT Roast beef, watercress
and horseradish brioche buns

Spinach focaccia with salmon and keta tartare

This open sandwich is visually stunning due to the contrast of colours, but more importantly it tastes amazing! This is true sophisticated baking – perfect for a celebratory occasion and worth all the effort. You need to ensure you use very fresh salmon for this recipe.

400g (14oz) skinless Scottish salmon fillet, finely diced

3–4 tbsp crème fraîche

70g (2½oz) capers, rinsed

2 tbsp finely chopped flat-leaf parsley

2 tbsp finely chopped dill, plus extra to garnish

100g (3½oz) keta (salmon roe)

freshly ground black pepper

For the focaccia

500g (1lb 2oz) strong white bread flour

2 tsp salt

2 x 7g sachets fast-action dried yeast

½ tsp freshly grated nutmeg

2 tbsp olive oil, plus extra for oiling and drizzling

300ml (½ pint) cold water

200g (7oz) spinach purée (see Tip)

sea salt flakes

First, make the focaccia. Put the flour, salt, yeast, nutmeg, oil and 250ml (9fl oz) of the water into a large bowl. Using your hands or a wooden spoon, gently combine to form a dough, then knead in the bowl for 5 minutes, gradually adding the remaining water and spinach purée.

Turn the dough out on to an oiled work surface and continue kneading for a further 5 minutes. Return the dough to the bowl, cover with clingfilm and leave to rise in a warm place for about 30 minutes, or until doubled in size.

Line 2 baking sheets, 20 x 26cm (8 x 10½in), with baking paper. Turn the dough out on to the work surface and divide into 2 equal pieces. Using your hands, press the dough into the prepared baking sheets, making sure it reaches into the corners. Cover with clingfilm and leave to rise for 1 hour.

Preheat the oven to 220°C (fan 200°C)/425°F/gas mark 7. Using your fingertips, create little dimples all over the focaccia, then drizzle with olive oil and add a good sprinkling of sea salt flakes. Bake in the oven for 20 minutes until golden. Drizzle with more oil while still hot, then transfer to cooling racks and leave to cool.

Meanwhile, put the salmon, crème fraiche, capers and herbs into a bowl and season with pepper. Mix well, then gently fold in the keta. Cover with clingfilm and chill in the refrigerator until required.

Cut the focaccia into 16 rectangles, each about 10 x 5cm (4 x 2in). Using 2 spoons, scoop a quenelle of salmon tartare on to each piece of bread. Garnish with dill and chill until ready to serve.

Tip ~ To make spinach purée, defrost 500g (1lb 2oz) frozen spinach and squeeze dry on kitchen paper or in a clean tea towel. Place in a blender and whizz to a purée.

Roast beef, watercress and horseradish brioche buns

There is something very satisfying about making your own bread and I especially like making brioche. These sweet, buttery buns combined with the rare roasted beef, the tangy sauce and crunchy watercress are simply divine.

100g (3½oz) crème fraîche

1 tbsp horseradish sauce

slightly salted butter, softened,
for spreading

handful of watercress

24 thin slices of rare roast beef (see Tip)

salt and freshly ground black pepper

For the brioche buns

125ml (4fl oz) warm water

1 x 7g sachet fast-action dried yeast

2 tbsp warm milk

2 tsp golden caster sugar

225g (8oz) strong white bread flour, plus
extra for dusting

1 tsp salt

1 tbsp unsalted butter, softened

1 large egg, beaten

beaten egg, to glaze

sesame seeds, for sprinkling

First, make the brioche buns. Put the 125ml (4fl oz) warm water, the yeast, warm milk and sugar into a bowl and leave to stand for 5 minutes until it starts to bubble.

Meanwhile, tip the flour and salt into a large bowl, add the butter and rub in using your fingertips until the mixture resembles fine breadcrumbs. Make a well in the centre of the flour and add the yeast mixture and egg. Using your hands, mix together until it forms a sticky dough – don't worry if the mixture feels a little wet at this stage, it will come together when kneading.

Knead the dough in the bowl for 10 minutes, stretching it up and out of the bowl with your hands – it will still be very sticky. The dough is ready when it feels soft and bouncy and will stretch up high without breaking. Cover the bowl with clingfilm and leave to rise in a warm place for about 30 minutes, or until doubled in size.

Line 2 baking sheets with baking paper. Knock back the dough by punching out the air, then turn out on to a lightly floured surface and knead for 2 minutes. Divide into 12 equal pieces,

then roll into balls and place on the prepared baking sheets. Loosely cover with a damp, clean tea towel and leave to rise for 30 minutes until doubled in size.

Preheat the oven to 200°C (fan 180°C)/400°F/gas mark 6. Brush the buns with the beaten egg and sprinkle with sesame seeds. Bake in the oven for 15–20 minutes, or until golden. Transfer to a cooling rack and leave to cool.

In a small bowl, mix the crème fraîche and horseradish together, then season to taste. Cut the brioche buns in half horizontally, then butter the cut sides. Spread over the horseradish cream, then add some watercress and 2 folded beef slices to each. Top with the brioche lids and serve.

Tip~If you wish to cook your own beef for this recipe, roast a 500g (1lb 2oz) beef topside joint in a preheated oven, 200°C (fan 180°C)/400°F/gas mark 6, for 15–20 minutes, then leave to cool before slicing.

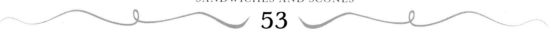

Serves 10–12 | **Preparation time:** 20 minutes, plus cooling and chilling | **Cooking time:** 15–20 minutes

Egg Florentine roulade

This is a great alternative to an egg sandwich; the spinach roulade is fluffy, light and moist and looks fabulous… the filling is just as exciting – chunky, creamy and zesty… your guests will definitely be asking for more.

250g (9oz) frozen spinach, defrosted, squeezed dry and chopped
5 eggs, separated
150g (5½oz) crème fraîche
50g (1¾oz) Greek yogurt
3 tbsp self-raising flour
salt and freshly ground black pepper

For the filling
4 eggs
4 tbsp mayonnaise
1 tsp Dijon mustard
1 punnet mustard cress
¼ tsp paprika

Preheat the oven to 180°C (fan 160°C)/350°F/gas mark 4. Line a 30 x 22cm (12 x 8½in) Swiss roll tin with baking paper.

Put the spinach, egg yolks, crème fraîche, yogurt and flour into a food processor and season well. Whizz until smooth, then transfer to a bowl. In a large, clean, dry bowl, whisk the egg whites to stiff peaks, then gently fold into the spinach mixture, taking care not to knock out too much air. Pour the mixture into the prepared tin, then tip the tin to make sure the mixture reaches the corners.

Bake in the oven for 15–20 minutes until lightly golden and firm to the touch. Turn out on to a clean tea towel lined with baking paper. Remove the baking paper from the sponge, then roll up from a long edge while still warm, using the paper underneath to help you. Leave to cool, covered with the tea towel.

Meanwhile, make the filling. Place the eggs in a saucepan and cover with cold water. Bring to the boil, then immediately remove from the heat. Cover with a lid and leave to stand in the hot water for 10–12 minutes. Drain, then cool under cold running water.

Shell the eggs and finely chop, then put into a bowl. Add the mayonnaise, mustard and cress and stir together well. Season with paprika, salt and pepper.

Unroll the roulade and, using a palette knife, evenly spread over the egg mixture. Re-roll the roulade tightly, then leave to firm up in the refrigerator for 1 hour. Cut into slices before serving.

Makes 16 | **Preparation time:** 25 minutes, plus marinating, curing and rising | **Cooking time:** 20 minutes

Vanilla-cured salmon on beetroot and caraway bread

I like experimenting with ingredients and as a pastry chef vanilla is my favourite flavour. Trust me, the sweetness of the vanilla and the smoky taste of the salmon really work well together, and the bread is slightly exotic, with a hint of fabulous pink from the beetroot. Use very fresh salmon for this recipe as it will take a couple of days to cure. You can make the bread the day before you want to serve it.

2 tsp vanilla bean paste
300g (10½oz) skinless salmon fillet
250ml (9fl oz) vodka
100g (3½oz) rock salt
70g (2½oz) muscovado sugar
1 tbsp mini capers, rinsed and chopped
1 tbsp chopped dill

freshly ground black pepper
½ lemon, to serve

For the beetroot bread
250g (9oz) strong white bread flour, plus extra for dusting
½ x 7g sachet fast-action dried yeast

½ tsp golden caster sugar
1 tsp caraway seeds
1 tsp salt
1 tbsp extra virgin olive oil, plus extra for greasing
125ml (4fl oz) warm water
70g (2½oz) cooked beetroot, puréed in a food processor

Rub the vanilla paste over the salmon fillet, then place in a deep non-reactive dish and pour over the vodka. Cover with clingfilm and leave to marinate in the refrigerator for at least 4 hours. Meanwhile, using a pestle and mortar, grind the salt and sugar together. Set aside.

Drain the marinade from the salmon, then rub the salt and sugar mixture into the salmon flesh. Cover with clingfilm and leave to cure in the refrigerator for 36–48 hours (the salt will extract the liquid from the fish).

Make the bread the day before the salmon is ready to serve. Put the flour into the bowl of a freestanding mixer fitted with a dough hook, make a well in the centre and add the dried yeast, sugar, caraway seeds, salt and extra virgin olive oil. Pour in the 125ml (4fl oz) water and the puréed beetroot and knead for 5 minutes. Cover the bowl with a clean tea towel and leave to rise in a warm place for about 30 minutes, or until it has doubled in size.

Turn the dough out on to a floured surface and divide into 2 equal pieces, then roll each into a rectangle. Roll up into log shapes to fit the tins, tucking the ends under. Transfer to 2 x 500g (1lb 2oz) greased loaf tins and leave to rise in a warm place for at least 20 minutes. Preheat the oven to 220°C (fan 200°C)/425°F/gas mark 7.

Bake the bread in the oven for about 20 minutes, or until it sounds slightly hollow when tapped on the base. Turn out on to a cooling rack and leave to cool completely. If baking the day before, store in an airtight container overnight.

When ready to serve, rinse the cured salmon under cold running water and pat dry with kitchen paper. Using a sharp knife, slice the salmon thinly. Cut the beetroot bread into 16 slices and cut the crusts off. Top each with slices of salmon and sprinkle over a few capers. Season with black pepper and garnish with the dill. Squeeze over the lemon before serving.

Herby lobster rolls

I was introduced to the lobster roll by Liz, my US publicist, during a meeting in a cool café in New York and I fell instantly in love with this New England favourite. Obviously the filling is amazing, but pan-frying the roll in golden butter is simply out of this world!

2 x 700–800g (1lb 9oz–1lb 12oz) cooked lobsters
good squeeze of lemon juice
1 celery stick, finely chopped
1 tbsp chopped chives
1 tbsp chopped dill, plus extra to garnish
2–3 tablespoons mayonnaise
50g (1¾oz) slightly salted butter
8 mini soft hot dog rolls
salt and freshly ground black pepper

Remove the meat from the tail, claws and knuckles of the lobsters, then roughly chop and put into a large bowl – you will need about 450g (1lb) lobster meat.

Add the lemon juice, celery, chives, dill and mayonnaise and mix together well, then season with salt and pepper.

Heat the butter in a large pan over a medium heat until it starts to smell nutty and the milk solids have turned lightly brown. Slice the buns vertically, but do not cut them all the way through. Open them out and add to the pan, cut sides down. Cook for 2 minutes until golden, then remove from the pan and leave to cool slightly.

Fill the rolls generously with the lobster mixture. Top each with a dill sprig and serve.

Tequila king prawn sliders

Bring a touch of Mexican fiesta to your afternoon tea with these spicy king prawns that are marinated in a zesty and boozy salsa. These prawns taste super fresh and are best served in a soft fluffy bread roll.

2 tbsp olive oil

1 small red onion, finely chopped

2 garlic cloves, crushed

20 raw peeled king prawns, with tails intact, deveined

3 tbsp tequila

1 tsp lime juice

10 small soft white mini rolls

extra virgin olive oil, for drizzling

salt and freshly ground black pepper

Preheat the oven to 200°C (fan 180°C)/400°F/gas mark 6.

Heat the olive oil in a large frying pan over a medium heat until it shimmers, then add the onion and garlic, season with salt and cook for about 8–10 minutes until softened and translucent.

Add the prawns and cook for about 3 minutes until they just turn pink. Remove the pan from the heat, add the tequila and scrape the bottom of the pan to incorporate any browned bits. Return to the heat and simmer until the smell of alcohol has cooked off and the prawns are cooked through. Remove from the heat, stir in the lime juice and season with salt and pepper to taste.

Meanwhile, cut the rolls in half horizontally and drizzle with a little extra virgin olive oil. Place the halves on a baking sheet and warm in the oven for about 5 minutes. Divide the prawns and all their juices among the roll bases, top with the lids and serve.

Paprika chicken ciabattas

This has to be my ultimate favourite sandwich. Delicious, juicy, smoky paprika-roasted chicken with peppery rocket, in ciabatta oozing with olive oil… believe me, it can be made in a larger size too!

2 free-range boneless, skinless chicken breasts, about 150g (5oz) each
2 tsp Worcestershire sauce
2 tsp smoked paprika
3 tbsp olive oil
150g (5½oz) cherry tomatoes (a mix of colours if available), halved
3 tbsp mayonnaise
8 mini ciabatta rolls or other small rolls
70g (2½oz) wild rocket leaves
salt and freshly ground black pepper

Place the chicken, Worcestershire sauce, 1 teaspoon of the smoked paprika and 2 tablespoons of the olive oil in a sealable freezer bag. Seal and give it a good shake, then leave to marinate in the refrigerator for 15 minutes.

Heat the remaining oil in a frying pan, add the marinated chicken and cook over a medium heat for 15–20 minutes, turning once, until cooked through but still succulent. Leave to rest for 10 minutes, then slice.

Meanwhile, heat the juices in the pan, add the cherry tomatoes and cook for 5 minutes until softened, then season and set aside.

In a small bowl, mix the mayonnaise and remaining smoked paprika together. Cut the ciabatta rolls in half, then spread a generous layer of the paprika mayonnaise over the bases. Divide the rocket among the bases, then pile up the chicken slices and add the cooked tomatoes. Spoon a good dollop of mayonnaise on to each, top with the lids and serve.

Tuna and pumpernickel 'mille feuille'

This little savoury mille feuille is created using layers of fine slices of bread and citrusy filling with an added aniseed crunch from the fresh fennel – a great savoury option for the healthier crowd.

440g can good-quality tuna in oil, drained
grated zest and juice of 1 lemon
2 tbsp capers, rinsed and chopped
2 tbsp chopped dill
1½ tbsp Dijon mustard

4 tbsp olive oil
1 large fennel bulb, trimmed and very thinly sliced
100g (3½oz) wild rocket leaves
18 rectangular slices of pumpernickel

slightly salted butter, softened, for spreading
salt and freshly ground black pepper

Put the tuna, lemon zest and juice, capers, dill, mustard and 2 tablespoons of the olive oil in a bowl, season well and mix together until the tuna has broken down and is thoroughly mixed.

In a separate bowl, mix the fennel, rocket and remaining olive oil together.

Butter each pumpernickel slice, then arrange some of the fennel salad on 6 slices and top with some of the tuna mixture. Cover each with a second layer of pumpernickel, butter side up, and repeat the salad and tuna layers. Top each with a final layer of pumpernickel, butter side down, to make 6 double sandwiches.

Cut each 'mille feuille' double sandwich into 3 and serve.

Cacao beef on pain perdu

Cacao or raw roasted cocoa beans have been used in savoury cooking for hundreds of years and are the perfect accompaniment to this rich fillet of beef. The French toast base is rich and sweet, making a deliciously perfect balance.

400g (14oz) beef fillet, or 2 x 200g (7oz) fillet steaks
2 pinches of salt
1 tbsp cacao nibs
1 tbsp vanilla bean paste

225ml (8fl oz) milk
3 eggs
small pinch of ground cinnamon
60g (2oz) unsalted butter

6 slices of brioche loaf, each cut into 2 x 5cm (2in) squares
freshly ground black pepper
olive oil, for drizzling
baby watercress or pea shoots, to garnish

Put the beef into a sealable freezer bag, then bash with a rolling pin or meat mallet until the meat is about 1cm (½in) thick. (Don't be too rough or you will shred the meat – the aim is to tenderize it.)

Remove the meat from the bag, place it on a chopping board and rub the salt, cacao nibs, vanilla bean paste and pepper on both sides. Return to the bag, seal and leave to marinate in the refrigerator for at least 2 hours, but preferably overnight.

In a shallow dish, mix the milk, eggs and cinnamon together. Heat half the butter in a large frying pan. Soak the brioche slices in the egg mixture for a few seconds, turning once. Carefully lift into the pan and, in batches if necessary, cook for 1–2 minutes on each side, or until golden brown. Remove from the pan and keep warm.

Heat the remaining butter in the pan until piping hot, it smells nutty and the milk solids have turned lightly brown. Add the marinated beef and cook for 30–60 seconds on each side until cooked to your liking but preferably still pink inside. Leave to rest for 5 minutes, then slice into thin squares the same size as the brioche.

Top the pain perdu with the beef slices and garnish with watercress or pea shoots. Drizzle with a little olive oil, then serve.

Slightly pickled vegetable bundles

I like to call these creations my little gardens! As well as being super cute they are so fresh and crunchy and I like to serve them with a rich satay sauce. Of course, you can use other seasonal vegetables or dipping sauces if you prefer.

200ml (7fl oz) white wine vinegar

150g (5½oz) caster sugar

1 tsp allspice berries

½ tsp yellow mustard seeds

1 tsp coriander seeds

1 bay leaf

6 baby carrots, with leaves on

6 large green asparagus stalks, trimmed

6 French breakfast radishes

1 large cucumber

mint sprigs, to garnish

ready-made satay sauce, to serve

Put the vinegar, sugar, spices and bay leaf in a small saucepan and heat gently until the sugar has dissolved. Place the carrots and asparagus in a heatproof, non-reactive shallow dish and pour over the hot vinegar. Leave to stand for 3 hours, then add the radishes and leave to stand for a further 1 hour. Rinse the vegetables and pat dry on kitchen paper.

Cut 6 long, thin slices from the cucumber using a speed peeler. Slice the pickled vegetables in half lengthways, then divide into 6 portions. Wrap a cucumber ribbon round each portion to create small bundles. Stand the bundles upright on a serving dish and garnish with mint sprigs. Serve with satay sauce.

Classic buttermilk scones

I had my first scone when I was seven years old on holiday in England when I discovered the joy of an afternoon tea. I have since tried many recipes over the years, but this version made with buttermilk is my favourite and the only one I use now.

225g (8oz) self-raising flour, plus extra for dusting
¼ tsp salt
25g (1oz) golden caster sugar
50g (1¾oz) unsalted butter, diced
125–150ml (4–5fl oz) buttermilk
4 tbsp milk
beaten egg, to glaze

Preheat the oven to 200°C (fan 180°C)/400°F/gas mark 6. Line a baking sheet with baking paper.

Sift the flour into a mixing bowl, then stir in the salt and sugar. Add the butter and rub in using your fingertips until the mixture resembles breadcrumbs. Mix the buttermilk and milk together in a jug. Pour the buttermilk into the bowl, a little at a time, and combine to form a smooth, but slightly sticky dough. Do not overmix.

Turn the dough out on to a very lightly floured surface and knead briefly (3–4 times only) to remove the cracks, then roll out to 3cm (1¼in) thick. Using a 5.5cm (2¼in) diameter plain cookie cutter, stamp out 16 scones (see Tip). Place on the prepared baking sheet and brush the tops with beaten egg.

Bake in the oven for 10–12 minutes until well risen and golden. Transfer to a cooling rack and leave to cool.

Tip~ I dip the cutter into a bowl of flour before stamping out each scone, so the dough doesn't stick to the cutter. Don't twist the cutter when pressing out the scones – this will ensure they rise straight and tall when baking in the oven.

Orange blossom and bee pollen scones

These scones have a touch of the Middle East with the addition of the floral scent of orange blossom extract and a rich honey flavour from the bee pollen. I like the way the dough turns a delicious yellow colour.

225g (8oz) self-raising flour, plus extra for dusting

¼ tsp salt

25g (1oz) golden caster sugar

50g (1¾oz) unsalted butter, diced

2 tsp orange blossom extract

125–150ml (4–5fl oz) buttermilk

4 tbsp milk

50g (1¾oz) bee pollen

beaten egg, to glaze

Preheat the oven to 200°C (fan 180°C)/400°F/gas mark 6. Line a baking sheet with baking paper.

Sift the flour into a mixing bowl, then stir in the salt and sugar. Add the butter and rub in using your fingertips until the mixture resembles breadcrumbs. Add the orange blossom extract. Mix the buttermilk and milk together in a jug. Pour the buttermilk into the bowl, a little at a time, and gently mix together. Before the dough has completely come together, add the bee pollen and combine to form a smooth, but slightly sticky dough. Do not overmix.

Turn the dough out on to a very lightly floured surface and knead briefly (3–4 times only) to remove the cracks, then roll out to 3cm (1¼in) thick. Using a 5.5cm (2¼in) diameter plain cookie cutter, stamp out 16 scones (see Tip on page 68). Place on the prepared baking sheet and brush the tops with beaten egg.

Bake in the oven for 10–12 minutes until well risen and golden. Transfer to a cooling rack and leave to cool.

LEFT Lemon scones
RIGHT Pistachio and rose scones

Lemon scones

If you like citrus flavours, this one is for you – it's absolutely perfect served with lemon curd or mascarpone cheese and a drizzle of Limoncello.

225g (8oz) self-raising flour, plus extra for dusting

¼ tsp salt

25g (1oz) golden caster sugar

50g (1¾oz) unsalted butter, diced

2 tsp lemon extract

grated zest of 1 large lemon

125–150ml (4–5fl oz) buttermilk

4 tbsp milk

beaten egg, to glaze

Preheat the oven to 200°C (fan 180°C)/400°F/gas mark 6. Line a baking sheet with baking paper.

Sift the flour into a mixing bowl, then stir in the salt and sugar. Add the butter and rub in using your fingertips until the mixture resembles breadcrumbs. Stir in the lemon extract and lemon zest. Mix the buttermilk and milk together in a jug. Pour the buttermilk into the bowl, a little at a time, and combine to form a smooth, but slightly sticky dough. Do not overmix.

Turn the dough out on to a very lightly floured surface and knead briefly (3–4 times only) to remove the cracks, then roll out to 3cm (1¼in) thick. Using a 5.5cm (2¼in) diameter plain cookie cutter, stamp out 16 scones (see Tip on page 68). Place on the prepared baking sheet and brush the tops with beaten egg.

Bake in the oven for 10–12 minutes until well risen and golden. Transfer to a cooling rack and leave to cool.

Pistachio and rose scones

These scones always remind me of walking through a Middle Eastern souk with all the gorgeous spices and dried edible flowers. I love serving these green beauties with a rose petal jelly.

225g (8oz) self-raising flour, plus extra for dusting

¼ tsp salt

25g (1oz) golden caster sugar

50g (1¾oz) unsalted butter, diced

2 tsp rose extract

125–150ml (4–5fl oz) buttermilk

4 tbsp milk

50g (1¾oz) shelled pistachio nuts, chopped

beaten egg, to glaze

Preheat the oven to 200°C (fan 180°C)/400°F/gas mark 6. Line a baking sheet with baking paper.

Sift the flour into a mixing bowl, then stir in the salt and sugar. Add the butter and rub in using your fingertips until the mixture resembles breadcrumbs. Add the rose extract. Mix the buttermilk and milk together in a jug. Pour the buttermilk into the bowl, a little at a time, and gently mix together. Before the dough has completely come together, add the pistachios and combine to form a smooth, but slightly sticky dough. Do not overmix.

Turn the dough out on to a very lightly floured surface and knead briefly (3–4 times only) to remove the cracks, then roll out to 3cm (1¼in) thick. Using a 5.5cm (2¼in) diameter plain cookie cutter, stamp out 16 scones (see Tip on page 68). Place on the prepared baking sheet and brush the tops with beaten egg.

Bake in the oven for 10–12 minutes until well risen and golden. Transfer to a cooling rack and leave to cool.

Raw cacao and raspberry scones

The combination of the raw roasted cacao and the sweet freeze-dried berries is a match made in heaven. Serve these with whipped cream and a very fruity raspberry preserve.

225g (8oz) self-raising flour, plus extra for dusting

¼ tsp salt

25g (1oz) golden caster sugar

50g (1¾oz) unsalted butter, diced

125–150ml (4–5fl oz) buttermilk

4 tbsp milk

10g (¼oz) freeze-dried raspberry pieces

20g (¾oz) cacao nibs

beaten egg, to glaze

Preheat the oven to 200°C (fan 180°C)/400°F/gas mark 6. Line a baking sheet with baking paper.

Sift the flour into a mixing bowl, then stir in the salt and sugar. Add the butter and rub in using your fingertips until the mixture resembles breadcrumbs. Mix the buttermilk and milk together in a jug. Pour the buttermilk into the bowl, a little at a time, and gently mix together. Before the dough has completely come together, add the raspberries and cacao nibs and combine to form a smooth, but slightly sticky dough. Do not overmix.

Turn the dough out on to a very lightly floured surface and knead briefly (3–4 times only) to remove the cracks, then roll out to 3cm (1¼in) thick. Using a 5.5cm (2¼in) diameter plain cookie cutter, stamp out 16 scones (see Tip on page 68). Place on the prepared baking sheet and brush the tops with beaten egg.

Bake in the oven for 10–12 minutes until well risen and golden. Transfer to a cooling rack and leave to cool.

Panettone scones

What makes these scones special is the addition of the whole pieces of candied citrus peel. It is very important to get whole peel and chop it yourself for that authentic taste.

225g (8oz) self-raising flour, plus extra for dusting

¼ tsp salt

25g (1oz) golden caster sugar

50g (1¾oz) unsalted butter, diced

2 tsp amaretto liqueur

125–150ml (4–5fl oz) buttermilk

4 tbsp milk

50g (1¾oz) candied peel, thinly chopped

beaten egg, to glaze

Preheat the oven to 200°C (fan 180°C)/400°F/gas mark 6. Line a baking sheet with baking paper.

Sift the flour into a mixing bowl, then stir in the salt and sugar. Add the butter and rub in using your fingertips until the mixture resembles breadcrumbs. Add the liqueur. Mix the buttermilk and milk together in a jug. Pour the buttermilk into the bowl, a little at a time, and gently mix together. Before the dough has completely come together, add the chopped candied peel and combine to form a smooth, but slightly sticky dough. Do not overmix.

Turn the dough out on to a very lightly floured surface and knead briefly (3–4 times only) to remove the cracks, then roll out to 3cm (1¼in) thick. Using a 5.5cm (2¼in) diameter plain cookie cutter, stamp out 16 scones (see Tip on page 68). Place on the prepared baking sheet and brush the tops with beaten egg.

Bake in the oven for 10–12 minutes until well risen and golden. Transfer to a cooling rack and leave to cool.

Makes 16 | **Preparation time:** 15 minutes, plus overnight soaking | **Cooking time:** 10–12 minutes

Aperol sultana scones

Bitter oranges are difficult to get hold of, but by using the classic aperitivo you bring their characteristic flavours to the ready-to-burst golden raisins, and your scones will take on a gorgeous orange colour. I like serving them with a fabulous French champagne jelly and cream.

225g (8oz) self-raising flour, plus extra for dusting

¼ tsp salt

25g (1oz) golden caster sugar

50g (1¾oz) unsalted butter, diced

2 tsp orange blossom extract

125–150ml (4–5fl oz) buttermilk

4 tbsp milk

50g (1¾oz) golden sultanas, soaked overnight in Aperol

beaten egg, to glaze

Preheat the oven to 200°C (fan 180°C)/400°F/gas mark 6. Line a baking sheet with baking paper.

Sift the flour into a mixing bowl, then stir in the salt and sugar. Add the butter and rub in using your fingertips until the mixture resembles breadcrumbs. Add the orange blossom extract. Mix the buttermilk and milk together in a jug. Pour the buttermilk into the bowl, a little at a time, and gently mix together. Before the dough has completely come together, add the sultanas and combine to form a smooth, but slightly sticky dough. Do not overmix.

Turn the dough out on to a very lightly floured surface and knead briefly (3–4 times only) to remove the cracks, then roll out to 3cm (1¼in) thick. Using a 5.5cm (2¼in) diameter plain cookie cutter, stamp out 16 scones (see Tip on page 68). Place on the prepared baking sheet and brush the tops with beaten egg.

Bake in the oven for 10–12 minutes until well risen and golden. Transfer to a cooling rack and leave to cool.

Makes 16 | **Preparation time:** 10 minutes | **Cooking time:** 15–20 minutes

Wholemeal scones

If you want an earthy afternoon tea, this recipe is for you. Packed with fibre,
I serve them with clotted cream and a good dollop of hazelnut spread
– really indulgent!

125g (4½oz) plain flour, plus extra for dusting
125g (4½oz) wholemeal flour
20g (¾oz) golden caster sugar
2 tsp baking powder
25g (1oz) butter, softened
1 egg, beaten
1 tsp vanilla bean paste
125–150ml (4–5fl oz) milk
150g (5½oz) plump golden sultanas
beaten egg, to glaze

Preheat the oven to 200°C (fan 180°C)/400°F/gas mark 6. Line a baking sheet with
baking paper.

In a large mixing bowl, stir the flours, sugar and baking powder together, then add the
softened butter, egg and vanilla paste. Add the milk, a little at a time, and gently mix
together. Before the dough has completely come together, add the sultanas and
combine to form a soft, but slightly sticky dough. Do not overmix.

Roll out the dough on a lightly floured surface to about 3cm (1¼in) thick. Using a
5.5cm (2¼in) diameter plain cookie cutter, stamp out 16 scones (see Tip on page 68).
Place on the prepared baking sheet and brush the tops with beaten egg.

Bake in the oven for 15–20 minutes until well risen and golden. Transfer to a cooling
rack and leave to cool.

Cheese scones

You can be as creative as you want with your choice of cheese and even go for colour by using Red Leicester. For me the best way to eat them is warm from the oven with lots of salted butter – yum!

225g (8oz) self-raising flour, plus extra for dusting
50g (1¾oz) unsalted butter, diced
50g (1¾oz) Cheddar cheese, grated
50g (1¾oz) Gruyère cheese, grated
2 tsp wholegrain mustard
100–125ml (3½–4fl oz) milk
beaten egg, to glaze

Preheat the oven to 200°C (fan 180°C)/400°F/gas mark 6. Line a baking sheet with baking paper.

Sift the flour into a large bowl. Add the butter and rub in with your fingertips until the mixture resembles fine breadcrumbs. Stir in three-quarters of the cheeses and all the mustard. Add the milk, a little at a time, and combine to form a smooth, but slightly sticky dough. Do not overmix.

Roll out the dough on a lightly floured surface to about 3cm (1¼in) thick. Using a 5.5cm (2¼in) diameter plain cookie cutter, stamp out 16 scones (see Tip on page 68). Place on the prepared baking sheet, brush the tops with beaten egg and sprinkle over the remaining cheese.

Bake in the oven for about 15 minutes until well risen and golden. Transfer to a cooling rack and leave to cool.

Cakes and sweet tarts

Spiced banana and walnut bundt cakes

Bundt cakes have had a huge revival in recent years and the special cake tins that make their distinctive shape are a real work of art – many are also collector's items. I really like these spiced banana bundt cakes – they are perfect for an afternoon tea and are super-yummy, as is the frosting. Remember, your bananas must be really ripe to get that great burst of flavour.

85g (3oz) unsalted butter, softened, plus extra for greasing

140g (5oz) self-raising flour, plus extra for dusting

115g (4oz) golden caster sugar

1 large egg, beaten

2 ripe bananas, chopped

pinch of salt

½ tsp ground ginger

½ tsp mixed spice

½ tsp bicarbonate of soda

100g (3½oz) walnuts, roasted and chopped (see Tip on page 17), plus extra to decorate

icing sugar, for dusting

For the frosting

25g (1oz) unsalted butter, softened

70g (2½oz) cream cheese

70g (2½oz) golden icing sugar

1 tsp vanilla bean paste

Preheat the oven to 180°C (fan 160°C)/350°F/gas mark 4. Grease and flour a 12-hole mini bundt cake tray.

In a large bowl, cream the butter and caster sugar together until pale and fluffy. Beat in the egg and bananas until smooth. Sift the flour, salt, spices and bicarbonate of soda together, then fold in. Stir in the walnuts.

Spoon the mixture into the prepared moulds, filling them about three-quarters full. Bake in the oven for 25 minutes until a skewer inserted into the centre comes out clean.

Leave to cool in the tin for 5 minutes, then turn out on to a cooling rack to cool completely.

To make the frosting, beat all the ingredients together until fluffy and smooth. Spoon into a piping bag fitted with a star-shaped piping nozzle and top each cooled cake with a swirl of frosting. Sprinkle over a few chopped walnuts and lightly dust with icing sugar before serving.

Gluten- and sugar-free carrot and coconut cake

At my pâtisserie Cake Boy we have a huge demand for gluten-free cakes, so I just had to work on creating some tasty recipes and this carrot cake is a winner! It's spicy, moist and very nutty with a decadent frosting. Stevia is a natural sweetener that also makes this cake sugar-free.

200g (7oz) unsalted butter, melted, plus extra for greasing

125g (4½oz) toasted desiccated coconut

125g (4½oz) pecan nuts, roasted and ground (see Tip on page 17), plus 100g (3½oz) roasted pecan halves, to decorate

50g (1¾oz) ground almonds

50g (1¾oz) rice flour

90g (3¼oz) stevia granules

pinch of salt

1 tsp baking powder

1½ tsp ground cinnamon, plus extra for dusting

4 eggs

2 tsp vanilla bean paste

300g (10½oz) grated carrots

splash of milk, if needed

For the frosting

600g (1lb 5oz) cream cheese

100g (3½oz) unsalted butter, softened

50g (1¾oz) stevia granules

pinch of ground cinnamon

2 tsp vanilla bean paste

1 tbsp milk

Preheat the oven to 160°C (fan 140°C)/325°F/gas mark 3. Grease 2 x 20cm (8in) diameter sandwich cake tins and line with baking paper.

In a large bowl, combine all the dry ingredients (I use a balloon whisk to do this). In a jug, beat the eggs, melted butter and vanilla paste until combined, then fold in the grated carrots. Pour the wet ingredients into the dry ingredients and mix well, adding a splash of milk if the mixture is too thick.

Divide the mixture between the prepared tins and bake in the oven for 25–30 minutes until golden and a skewer inserted into the centre comes out clean. Leave to cool in the tins for 10 minutes, then turn out on to a cooling rack to cool completely.

To make the frosting, beat all the ingredients together until creamy and fluffy. Secure one of the cooled cakes on your cake stand with a little of the frosting, then spread a good layer over the top of the cake and sandwich together with the second cake. Using a palette knife, cover the cake completely with the remaining frosting. Decorate with the pecan halves and a light dusting of cinnamon.

Pistachio and rose financiers

Traditionally made with ground almonds, for these financiers I substituted ground pistachios to make the recipe moreish and colourful. The rose cream topping and edible rose petals bring a Middle Eastern touch to this delicate tea time treat.

150g (5½oz) unsalted butter
85g (3oz) shelled pistachio nuts, plus extra to decorate
70g (2½oz) plain flour
6 egg whites
pinch of salt
175g (6oz) icing sugar, sifted
50g (1¾oz) ground almonds

To decorate
200ml (7fl oz) whipping cream
1 tbsp vanilla sugar
few drops of rose extract, to taste
edible dried rose petals or buds

Heat the butter in small saucepan and bubble until it smells nutty and the milk solids turn golden brown. Set aside.

Put the pistachios and flour into a food processor and whizz until finely ground. In a large bowl, whisk the egg whites and salt together until foamy, then fold in the icing sugar, flour mixture and ground almonds. Fold in the melted beurre noisette. Pour the mixture into a piping bag and leave to firm up in the refrigerator for at least 1 hour.

Preheat the oven to 180°C (fan 160°C)/350°F/gas mark 4. Pipe the mixture into 24 small financier moulds (or you can use mini muffin tins) and bake in the oven for 15–20 minutes until lightly golden brown. Leave to cool in the trays for 15 minutes, then turn out on to a cooling rack to cool completely.

To decorate, lightly whip the whipping cream, vanilla sugar and rose extract, then spoon into a piping bag fitted with a medium star- or petal-shaped piping nozzle. Pipe rosettes on to each financier and decorate with extra chopped pistachios and dried rose petals or buds.

Gluten-free chocolate cake

Chocolate has always been my ingredient of choice and you don't have to be on a gluten-free diet to enjoy this rich and dark creation – all my customers love it!

115g (4oz) butter, melted, plus extra for greasing
350g (12oz) ground almonds
25g (1oz) desiccated coconut
100g (3½oz) unsweetened cocoa powder
70g (2½oz) stevia granules
2 tsp baking powder

1 tsp salt
225ml (8fl oz) milk
3 large eggs
2 tsp vanilla bean paste
2 tbsp clear honey
cacao nibs, to decorate

For the ganache
350g (12oz) dark chocolate (80% cocoa solids), roughly chopped
125ml (4fl oz) double cream
2 tsp vanilla bean paste

Preheat the oven to 170°C (fan 140°C)/325°F/gas mark 3. Grease 2 x 20cm (8in) diameter sandwich cake tins and line with baking paper.

In a large bowl, combine all the dry ingredients together. In a separate bowl, combine all the wet ingredients, then fold into the dry ingredients, being careful not to overmix.

Divide the mixture between the prepared tins and bake in the oven for 30–40 minutes until a skewer inserted into the centre comes out clean. Leave to cool in the tins for 10 minutes, then turn out on to a cooling rack to cool completely.

To make the ganache, melt the chocolate in a heatproof bowl set over a saucepan of barely simmering water, making sure the surface of the water does not touch the bowl. Meanwhile, put the cream into a saucepan and heat to just below boiling point. Remove the melted chocolate from the heat and slowly pour in the cream, gently stirring with a balloon whisk until smooth and glossy. Fold in the vanilla paste. Leave to cool and thicken to a spreadable, glossy ganache.

When thickened, spread a good layer of ganache on to one of the cakes, then sandwich together with the remaining cake. Spread the remaining ganache over the top of the cake and decorate with cacao nibs.

Orange marmalade squares

There is something very comforting about marmalade and, of course, something very British, which I love. This easy-to-bake cake is perfect for tea time or as a little lunch box treat.

175g (6oz) unsalted butter, softened, plus extra for greasing
175g (6oz) golden caster sugar
3 eggs
250g (9oz) self-raising flour
3 tbsp milk
2 tbsp orange liqueur, such as Cointreau or Grand Marnier
2 tbsp thick-cut marmalade

To decorate
6 tbsp thick-cut marmalade
apricot glaze (see Tip on page 94)

Preheat the oven to 180°C (fan 160°C)/350°F/gas mark 4. Grease a rectangular brownie tin, about 18 x 31cm (7 x 12½in), and line with baking paper.

In a large bowl, cream the butter and sugar together until pale and fluffy. Beat in the eggs one at the time, beating well between each addition. Sift the flour, then fold in. Mix in the milk, liqueur and marmalade.

Spoon the mixture into the prepared tin and spread evenly. Bake in the oven for 30 minutes until golden and a skewer inserted into the centre comes out clean. Leave to cool in the tin for 10 minutes, then turn out on to a cooling rack to cool completely.

To decorate, spread a thick layer of marmalade all over the cake (if very thick, warm it first in a saucepan to make it easier to spread), then brush over a thin layer of apricot glaze. Cut into 12 squares or fingers to serve.

Orange and cranberry nutty tea loaf

At my pâtisserie Cake Boy in London we sell hundreds of loaf cakes every week – people love them because they look homemade. This cake with its wintery flavours of orange and cranberry is a popular choice when the weather gets colder.

175g (6oz) unsalted butter, softened, plus extra for greasing
175g (6oz) golden caster sugar
3 eggs
250g (9oz) self-raising flour
finely grated zest of 2 oranges and a squeeze of juice
100g (3½oz) fresh or frozen cranberries, chopped
100g (3½oz) hazelnuts, roasted and chopped (see Tip on page 17)

Preheat the oven to 170°C (fan 140°C)/325°F/gas mark 3. Grease a 20 x 11cm (8 x 4¼in) loaf tin and line with baking paper.

In a large bowl, cream the butter and sugar together until pale and fluffy. Beat in the eggs, one at a time, then sift in the flour and add the orange zest and juice. Mix until well blended. Stir in the cranberries and nuts.

Spoon the mixture into the prepared loaf tin and bake in the oven for 50–60 minutes, or until a skewer inserted into the centre comes out clean. Leave to cool in the tin for 10 minutes, then turn out on to a cooling rack to cool completely. Wrap in clingfilm and store overnight – the flavour will only improve the next day.

Scandinavian apple cake

Scandinavian baking has now been put back on the map and I am a big fan.
This rich, spicy apple cake is delicious served warm with a sweet vanilla custard.

150g (5½oz) unsalted butter, melted and
cooled, plus extra for greasing
5 firm apples, such as Granny Smith or Cox
150g (5½oz) light muscovado sugar
2 eggs
300g (10½oz) plain flour

2 tsp baking powder
1 tsp mixed spice
1 tsp ground cinnamon
½ tsp freshly grated nutmeg
200g (7oz) golden sultanas

100g (3½oz) walnuts, roasted and chopped
(see Tip on page 17)
4 tbsp apple brandy (optional)
apricot glaze (see Tip), to decorate
sifted icing sugar, for dusting

Preheat the oven to 180°C (fan 160°C)/350°F/gas mark 4.
Grease a 20cm (8in) diameter springform cake tin and line
with baking paper.

Peel and grate all but 1 of the apples into a bowl, add the sugar
and cooled butter and combine. Add the eggs and mix well.
Sift the dry ingredients, then add to the apple mixture and
fold in. Stir in the sultanas, walnuts and brandy, if using.

Pour the mixture into the prepared tin. Peel and slice the
remaining apple, then arrange on top of the cake in a neat circle.

Bake in the oven for 50–60 minutes until golden and a skewer
inserted into the centre comes out clean. (The cake will be very
moist, but that's normal.) Leave to cool in the tin for 5 minutes,
then transfer to a cooling rack.

Brush with a little apricot glaze and leave to cool, then serve
with a light dusting of icing sugar.

Tip ~ To achieve a professional, glossy finish on cakes and tarts,
use apricot glaze. To make the glaze, put some apricot jam into a
small saucepan and gently warm through, then press through a
fine sieve to remove any lumps. Using a pastry brush, brush the
warm glaze over the finished cake or tart and leave to cool.

Mini upside-down pineapple cakes

If you fancy a touch of 1970s retro chic, this cake is for you, but there's no tinned pineapple in sight. I use fresh pineapple roasted with lashings of dark rum and coconut, making a great little dessert for an afternoon tea – with a touch of nostalgia.

125g (4½oz) unsalted butter, softened, plus extra for greasing

50g (1¾oz) light muscovado sugar

400g (14oz) peeled, cored and cubed ripe pineapple (about 1 small pineapple)

3 tsp desiccated coconut

2 tbsp dark rum

70g (2½oz) natural glacé cherries, quartered

100g (3½oz) golden caster sugar

2 eggs

100g (3½oz) self-raising flour

1 tsp baking powder

1 tsp vanilla bean paste

apricot glaze (see Tip on page 94), to decorate

Preheat the oven to 180°C (fan 160°C)/350°F/gas mark 4. Grease 4 x 250ml (9fl oz) ramekins and line the bases with baking paper.

Heat 25g (1 oz) of the butter and the muscovado sugar in a frying pan and stir until melted, then add the pineapple cubes. Cook for about 5 minutes, or until golden and caramelized. Add the desiccated coconut and rum and cook until the liquid has evaporated. Remove from the heat and add the glacé cherries. Mix well and set aside.

In a large bowl, cream the remaining butter and the caster sugar together until pale and fluffy. Beat in the eggs, one at a time, beating well after each addition. Sift the flour and baking powder together, then fold in. Stir in the vanilla paste and most of the pineapple mixture.

Spoon the remaining pineapple into the prepared ramekins, then spoon the cake mixture over the top. Bake in the oven for 35–40 minutes until golden and risen. Leave to cool in the ramekins for 15 minutes, then turn out on to a serving plate. For a glossy finish, brush the little cakes with apricot glaze. These can be served warm or cold.

Serves 10 | **Preparation time:** 20 minutes | **Cooking time:** about 1 hour

Candied apricot cake

I was inspired to create this recipe during a trip to the Atlas mountains in Morocco, where apricots grow in abundance. The combination of the baked fruits with orange blossom is luscious and the glorious green from the pistachios offers a lovely contrast to this easy, but impressive cake.

200g (7oz) unsalted butter, softened, plus extra for greasing
2 x 411g cans apricots in natural juice
225g (8oz) golden caster sugar
finely grated zest of 2 oranges
2 eggs
2 tsp orange blossom extract
300g (10½oz) self-raising flour
175ml (6fl oz) milk
60g (2¼oz) icing sugar
150g (5½oz) shelled pistachio nuts, roasted and chopped (see Tip on page 17), to decorate

Preheat the oven to 180°C (fan 160°C)/350°F/gas mark 4. Grease a 20cm (8in) square, 5cm (2in) deep cake tin and line with baking paper.

Drain the apricots, reserving 200ml (7fl oz) of the juice. Pat the apricots dry with kitchen paper, then arrange, cut side up, in the bottom of the prepared tin.

In a large bowl, cream the butter, caster sugar and orange zest together until pale and fluffy. Beat in the eggs, one at a time, then add the orange blossom extract and sift in half the flour. Stir in half the milk. Repeat with the remaining flour and milk.

Spoon the mixture over the apricots and level the top. Bake in the oven for 55 minutes, or until a skewer inserted into the centre comes out clean. Leave in the tin.

Meanwhile, put the icing sugar and reserved juice in a saucepan and cook over a low heat, stirring, for 5 minutes, or until the sugar has dissolved. Increase the heat to high and bring to the boil, then boil, without stirring, for 4–5 minutes, or until the mixture thickens. Pour the syrup over the warm cake and leave in the tin until completely cold. Remove the cake from the tin and place on a serving plate. Sprinkle with the pistachios before serving.

Coffee and walnut cake

I fell in love with coffee and walnut cake when I moved to the UK, where it is almost a national treasure. Here I have dared to lighten the recipe to make it fresher and creamier – I can guarantee you will want seconds!

200g (7oz) unsalted butter, softened, plus extra for greasing

200g (7oz) golden caster sugar

4 eggs, beaten

200g (7oz) self-raising flour

3 tbsp instant coffee, dissolved in 1 tbsp boiling water and cooled

70g (2½oz) walnuts, roasted and chopped (see Tip on page 17), plus extra halves to decorate

For the frosting

500g (1lb 2oz) mascarpone cheese

100g (3½oz) golden icing sugar

1–2 tbsp coffee liqueur

Preheat the oven to 170°C (fan 140°C)/325°F/gas mark 3. Grease 2 x 20cm (8in) diameter sandwich cake tins and line with baking paper.

In a large bowl, beat the butter, caster sugar, eggs and flour together until smooth and fluffy using an electric hand whisk. Beat in the cold coffee, then fold in the chopped walnuts.

Divide the mixture between the prepared tins and bake in the oven for 25–30 minutes until well risen and golden, and a skewer inserted into the centre comes out clean. Leave to cool in the tins for 5 minutes, then turn out on to a cooling rack to cool completely.

To make the frosting, beat all the ingredients together until smooth. Spoon about 4 tablespoons of frosting into a piping bag and set aside. Sandwich the cooled cakes together with one-third of the remaining frosting, then cover the top and sides of the cake with the rest. Pipe more frosting around the rim and on top, then arrange the walnut halves over the top and sides to decorate. Chill in the refrigerator until ready to serve.

Clementine and pomegranate cake

This is my alternative to a Christmas cake. It's really stunning, with beautiful jewel-like pomegranate seeds that look like rubies. This is a very moist cake and uses whole fruits to ensure it is packed with festive flavours… it also happens to be gluten and dairy free!

4 clementines or satsumas, unpeeled

1 cinnamon stick

oil, for greasing

6 large eggs

225g (8oz) light muscovado sugar

1 tsp gluten-free baking powder

300g (10½oz) ground almonds

For the syrup

1 pomegranate, halved

25g (1oz) light muscovado sugar

1 tsp orange blossom extract

1 tsp vanilla bean paste

To decorate

3 tbsp apricot glaze (see Tip on page 94)

icing sugar, for dusting

Put the clementines or satsumas and cinnamon stick into a medium saucepan, cover with cold water and bring to the boil. Reduce the heat, cover with a lid and simmer for 1–1½ hours, then drain the fruit and remove the cinnamon stick. Leave to cool for 30 minutes, then halve the cooked fruit and discard the pips. Put the fruit, including the peel, into a blender or food processor and blend to a purée. Set aside.

Preheat the oven to 180°C (fan 160°C)/350°F/gas mark 4. Grease a 23cm (9in) diameter, 9cm (3½in) deep cake tin and line with baking paper. Using an electric hand whisk, whisk the eggs and sugar in a heatproof bowl over a saucepan of barely simmering water for about 5 minutes until pale and mousse-like. Take the bowl off the heat and add the baking powder, ground almonds and the fruit purée. Fold in gently but thoroughly.

Spoon the mixture into the prepared tin and bake in the oven for 20 minutes. Reduce the oven temperature to 160°C (fan 140°C)/325°F/gas mark 3 and bake for a further 30 minutes,

or until a skewer inserted into the centre comes out clean. Leave to cool in the tin for 15 minutes, then transfer to a cooling rack to cool completely.

To make the syrup, squeeze the pomegranate halves to extract the juice, reserving the seeds, then pour the juice into a small saucepan. Add the sugar and bring to the boil, then simmer for 2 minutes. Leave to cool slightly (the liquid should still be warm), then stir in the orange blossom extract and vanilla paste. Using a pastry brush, 'soak' the cake with the warm pomegranate syrup and leave in the tin until completely cold.

Remove the cold cake from the tin and place on a serving plate. Brush the apricot glaze all over the cake, including the sides. Just before serving, scatter the reserved pomegranate seeds over the top of the cake and dust with icing sugar.

Light Italian fruit cake

I do like a piece of fruit cake when sitting down to an afternoon tea, but sometimes it can be a little bit too rich and dense, so this light Italian version is perfect as it is not too dense. Make sure to use good-quality candied citrus peel and very plump dried fruits for a perfect result.

200g (7oz) self-raising flour
175g (6oz) unsalted butter, softened
175g (6oz) light muscovado sugar
3 large eggs
2 tbsp milk
2 tbsp amaretto liqueur
300g (10½oz) mixed dried fruit, such as raisins, sultanas and currants
50g (1¾oz) candied peel, chopped
50g (1¾oz) glacé cherries, chopped

To decorate
4 tbsp apricot glaze (see Tip on page 94)
assorted glacé fruits

Preheat the oven to 180°C (fan 160°C)/350°F/gas mark 4. Line the base and sides of a 20cm (8in) square cake tin with baking paper.

Sift the flour into a bowl. In a separate large bowl, cream the butter and sugar together until pale and fluffy, then beat in the eggs, one at a time, adding a little of the flour after each addition. Fold in the remaining flour, the milk and the amaretto. Add the dried fruit, candied peel and cherries and mix together until well combined.

Spoon the mixture into the prepared tin and level the top. Bake in the oven for 1 hour 30 minutes, or until a skewer inserted into the centre comes out clean. Leave to cool completely in the tin.

Brush the apricot glaze over the top and sides of the cake. Decorate with the glacé fruits, then brush over more glaze. Store in an airtight container.

French flourless cake

Every time I make this cake I feel proud to be French. It is rich in chocolate, making it really decadent, and being a rustic-style cake there's no need to worry about the presentation or decoration – all that is needed is plenty of crème fraîche served on the side. This cake is sure to become one of your classic recipes!

200g (7oz) unsalted butter, plus extra for greasing
200g (7oz) dark chocolate, 70% cocoa solids, roughly chopped
2 tbsp Cognac
4 eggs, separated
225g (8oz) golden caster sugar

Preheat the oven to 180°C (fan 160°C)/350°F/gas mark 4. Grease a 23cm (9in) diameter springform cake tin and line with baking paper.

Melt the butter, chocolate and Cognac together in a heatproof bowl set over a saucepan of barely simmering water, making sure the surface of the water does not touch the bowl. Leave to cool for a few minutes.

In a large bowl, whisk the egg yolks and half the sugar together using an electric hand whisk until very pale and fluffy. Fold in the melted chocolate mixture.

In a separate large, clean, dry bowl, whisk the egg whites to soft peaks, then add the remaining sugar a little at a time and whisk until stiff. Using a rubber spatula, gently fold into the chocolate mixture until smooth.

Spoon the mixture into the prepared tin and bake in the oven for 40 minutes, or until a skewer inserted into the centre comes out clean. Leave to cool completely in the tin.

Tip ~ This cake is quite sticky, so be careful when removing it from the tin.

Fresh fig cake

I always try to bake with seasonal ingredients both at work and at home, and I can't wait for the fig season as I simply love them. In this cake, the fruits are baked in the batter and the finished cake is drenched in a sweet cinnamon and orange syrup.

125g (4½oz) unsalted butter, melted, plus extra for greasing

4 eggs

150g (5½oz) icing sugar, plus extra for dusting

100g (3½oz) plain flour

1 tsp baking powder

150g (5½oz) ground almonds

9 just ripe fresh figs, halved

For the syrup

200ml (7fl oz) orange juice

70g (2½oz) golden caster sugar

1 tsp ground cinnamon

Preheat the oven to 180°C (fan 160°C)/350°F/gas mark 4. Grease a 23cm (9in) diameter springform cake tin and line with baking paper.

In a large bowl, whisk the eggs and icing sugar together using an electric hand whisk until pale and fluffy. Sift the flour and baking powder together, then fold in with the almonds. Add the melted butter and mix together until smooth.

Spoon the mixture into the prepared tin and level the top. Arrange the figs, cut sides up, over the surface. Bake in the oven for 35 minutes, or until a skewer inserted into the centre comes out clean. Leave to cool in the tin for 10 minutes.

Meanwhile, put the orange juice, caster sugar and cinnamon into a small saucepan and heat over a low heat for 10 minutes until they form a syrup. Pour over the slightly warm cake and leave to cool completely.

Remove the cake from the tin and lightly dust with icing sugar to finish.

Triple marble bundt cake

I am very proud of my vintage bundt cake tin, as it produces an amazing centrepiece cake every time. This particular cake offers a spectacular surprise – when cut, you will discover a trio of flavours and colours that provide a wow factor for your guests.

250g (9oz) unsalted butter, plus extra
for greasing

325g (11½oz) plain flour, plus extra
for dusting

350g (12oz) golden caster sugar

5 eggs

2 tsp vanilla bean paste

2 tsp baking powder

2 tbsp milk, plus extra if needed

20g (¾oz) unsweetened cocoa powder

1 tbsp raspberry extract

2 tsp red food colouring

For the icing

150g (5½oz) icing sugar

juice of 1 lemon

Preheat the oven to 160°C (fan 140°C)/325°F/gas mark 3. Generously grease and flour a 22cm (8½in) bundt cake tin.

In a large bowl, cream the butter and sugar together until very pale and fluffy. Beat in the eggs, one at a time, beating well after each addition, then add the vanilla paste. Sift the flour and baking powder together, then fold in, adding a little splash of milk if the mixture is too stiff.

Divide the vanilla cake mixture into 3 separate bowls. Mix the cocoa powder and milk into one, and the raspberry extract and food colouring into another. Leave the third one plain.

Spoon the plain vanilla mixture into the prepared tin, followed by the red raspberry mixture, and finally the chocolate mixture. Using the blade of a knife, create waves in the batter to form a marble effect.

Bake in the oven for 45 minutes, or until a skewer inserted into the centre comes out clean. Leave to cool in the tin for 15 minutes.

Meanwhile, make the icing. Put the icing sugar and lemon juice into a bowl and mix together.

Turn the cake out on to a serving plate and pour over the icing while the cake is warm. Leave to stand for at least 2 hours before serving.

Serves 12 | **Preparation time:** 15 minutes | **Cooking time:** 1 hour

Sticky pecan cake

This is American baking at its best. Packed with unrefined sugars, maple syrup, sweet cinnamon, juicy apples and crunchy pecans, this cake is topped with ruby apples and drenched in a buttery syrup…heaven!

140g (5oz) unsalted butter, melted, plus extra for greasing

200g (7oz) light muscovado sugar

150g (5½oz) pure maple syrup

1 tsp ground cinnamon

½ tsp ground cloves

½ tsp ground ginger

2 large eggs, beaten

2 tbsp milk

250g (9oz) plain flour

1½ tsp baking powder

½ tsp salt

2 red apples

250g (9oz) pecan nut halves, roasted and chopped (see Tip on page 17)

For the glaze

1 tbsp unsalted butter, melted

2 tbsp pure maple syrup

Preheat the oven to 180°C (fan 160°C)/350°F/gas mark 4. Grease a 23cm (9in) diameter springform cake tin and line with baking paper.

In a large bowl, mix the melted butter, sugar, syrup and spices together. Stir in the eggs and milk. Sift the flour, baking powder and salt together, then fold in until the mixture is well combined. Peel, core and dice 1 apple, then fold in.

Spoon the mixture into the prepared tin. Core and dice the remaining apple, leaving the skin on. Scatter over the mixture with the pecans. Bake in the oven for 50 minutes.

Meanwhile, mix the glaze ingredients together. Remove the cake from the oven, brush over the maple glaze, then return to the oven and continue to cook for another 10 minutes, or until a skewer inserted into the centre comes out clean.

Leave to cool in the tin for 15 minutes, then turn out on to a cooling rack to cool completely.

Strawberry ombré cake

This gorgeous cake simply shouts celebration! Under the pastel frosting you will find a moist vanilla sponge layered with strawberry conserve and more creamy frosting. It is a delicious showstopper that you are going to love to make and serve.

225g (8oz) unsalted butter, softened, plus extra for greasing
225g (8oz) golden caster sugar
4 large eggs, beaten
2 tsp vanilla bean paste
2 tbsp milk
225g (8oz) self-raising flour
1 tsp baking powder

For the filling
425ml (15fl oz) whipping cream
70g (2½oz) vanilla sugar
strawberry preserve

For the frosting
100g (3½oz) cream cheese (the drier, the better – I use Philadelphia)
100g (3½oz) unsalted butter, softened
1 tsp vanilla extract
400g (14oz) icing sugar
red food colouring

Preheat the oven to 180°C (fan 160°C)/350°F/gas mark 4. Grease 2 x 20cm (8in) diameter sandwich cake tins and line the bases with baking paper.

In a large mixing bowl, beat the butter until pale and light. Add the sugar and cream together until the mixture is pale and fluffy. Beat in the eggs a spoonful at a time, beating well after each addition. Add the vanilla paste and milk and stir in. Sift the flour and baking powder together, then fold in.

Divide the mixture equally between the prepared tins. Gently tap the tins on the work surface to expel any large air pockets and level the tops. Bake in the oven for 25–30 minutes, or until golden and a skewer inserted into the centre comes out clean. Turn out on to a cooling rack and leave to cool completely.

When the cakes are completely cold, slice each in half horizontally. Whip the cream until it holds its shape, then fold in the vanilla sugar. Spread a layer of strawberry preserve over the 2 bases, then spread a layer of cream over each. Spread a layer of cream only over the remaining 2 cake halves. Sandwich 2 halves together on a serving plate, starting with a jam and cream layer, followed by a cream-only layer. Repeat the layers. Chill in the refrigerator for 2 hours before decorating.

Meanwhile, make the frosting. In a large bowl, beat together the cream cheese and butter until soft and creamy. Stir in the vanilla extract, then sift the icing sugar and gradually mix in. Divide the frosting between 4 small bowls. Leaving one bowl of frosting uncoloured, add different amounts of red food colouring to the other 3 bowls to form different shades of frosting (see picture). Transfer each to a separate piping bag fitted with a large star-shaped piping nozzle.

To decorate, use a palette knife to cover the cake all over with a thin layer of the uncoloured frosting, saving some for the final decoration. Starting with the darkest-coloured frosting, pipe large circular rosettes around the base of the cake. Take the next darkest frosting and pipe another row of rosettes above the first row. Use the palest-coloured frosting to pipe a final row of rosettes to cover the top of the cake. Use the remaining uncoloured frosting to add a few smaller rosettes on the top and edges of the cake. Chill in the refrigerator for 1 hour before serving.

Tip~ Make sure that the eggs, butter and cream cheese are at room temperature before you begin.

LEFT Matcha and lemon cake
RIGHT Chocolate and ginger tart

Matcha and lemon cake

Green tea is very popular in Japan, not only for drinking, but in baking too.
As well as the striking colour, the green tea lends a subtle flavour to the cake
that works very well with the zesty white chocolate topping.

20g (¾oz) unsalted butter, melted, plus
extra for greasing
60g (2¼oz) plain flour
10g (¼oz) cornflour
2 tbsp matcha green tea powder
2 tbsp milk
4 eggs, separated

70g (2½oz) golden caster sugar
fresh raspberries, to decorate

For the white chocolate and lemon cream
grated zest and juice of 2 lemons
100g (3½oz) golden caster sugar

4 tsp Limoncello liqueur (optional)
200g (7oz) white chocolate, chopped
400g (14oz) unsalted butter, softened
150g (5½oz) golden icing sugar, plus extra
for dusting

Preheat the oven to 180°C (fan 160°C)/350°F/gas mark 4.
Grease a 20cm (8in) diameter loose-bottomed sandwich cake tin
and line with baking paper.

Put the flour, cornflour and matcha powder into a bowl and mix
together. In a separate bowl, mix the melted butter and milk
together. Set aside.

In a large, clean dry bowl, whisk the egg whites to stiff peaks,
adding the sugar a little at a time. Add the egg yolks, one at a
time, beating well after each addition. Using a rubber spatula,
fold in the flour mixture until combined, then add the melted
butter mixture and fold in.

Spoon the mixture into the prepared tin and bake in the oven
for about 15–20 minutes, or until a skewer inserted into the
centre comes out clean. Turn out on to a cooling rack and
leave to cool completely.

Meanwhile, put the lemon juice and sugar in a saucepan and
bring to the boil, stirring until the sugar has dissolved. Add the
Limoncello, if using, and bring to the boil again. Remove from
the heat and mix in the white chocolate, stirring until it has
melted. Leave to cool.

In a separate large bowl, cream the butter and icing sugar
together until pale and fluffy. Mix in the cooled chocolate
mixture and beat for a further minute. Spoon the cream into a
piping bag fitted with a 2cm (¾in) diameter plain piping nozzle.

Place the matcha sponge on a serving plate, then pipe the cream
over the top. Decorate with raspberries and serve dusted
with icing sugar.

Chocolate and ginger tart

There is no pastry in this tart – instead the crust is made of crushed ginger biscuits pressed into the base of the tin and baked in a hot oven to give it extra crunch and flavour. The filling is a combination of a baked rich chocolate custard with stem ginger. This is absolutely amazing when served warm with a lot of whipped cream.

For the base
350g (12oz) ginger biscuits
70g (2½oz) unsalted butter, melted

For the filling
470ml (17fl oz) milk
150g (5½oz) dark chocolate, 70% cocoa solids, chopped
3 egg yolks

100g (3½oz) golden caster sugar
60g (2¼oz) cornflour
2 tsp vanilla bean paste
pinch of salt
3 balls of stem ginger, chopped

Preheat the oven to 180°C (fan 160°C)/350°F/gas mark 4. Grease a 20cm (8in) diameter, 4cm (1½in) deep fluted tart tin.

To make the base, put the biscuits into a food processor and whizz to form crumbs, then add the melted butter and combine. Tip into the prepared tin. Using a spoon and your fingers, smooth out the crumbs to form an even layer in the bottom and up the sides of the tin. Bake in the oven for 10 minutes, then leave to cool completely.

To make the filling, put the milk and chocolate in a medium heavy-based saucepan and heat gently until the chocolate is melted.

In a heatproof bowl, whisk the egg yolks, sugar, cornflour, vanilla paste and salt together until pale and fluffy. Gradually whisk in the chocolate mixture, then pour the custard into a jug.

Cover the cooled biscuit base with the chopped stem ginger, then pour over the custard right up to the edges of the tin. Bake in the oven for 30–35 minutes until set. Remove from the tin on to a serving plate and leave to cool, then chill in the refrigerator for a couple of hours. Serve at room temperature with lots of whipped cream, if liked.

Makes 6 large or 12 small tartlets | **Preparation time:** 20 minutes, plus chilling and cooling | **Cooking time:** 30 minutes

Tartelettes aux fruits

I am always mesmerized by the displays of fruit tarts in the windows of pâtisseries when I go home to France. They are actually incredibly simple to make, but they need to be made properly; the pastry must be short and buttery, the crème pâtissière must be creamy, and the fruits should be sweet and ripe… and, of course, look gorgeous!

For the pastry
250g (9oz) plain flour, plus extra for dusting
1 tsp golden caster sugar
pinch of salt
125g (4½oz) cold unsalted butter, diced, plus extra for greasing
2–3 tbsp cold water

For the crème pâtissière
600ml (20fl oz) milk
5 egg yolks
100g (3½oz) golden caster sugar
50g (1¾oz) custard powder
1 tsp vanilla bean paste
2 tsp orange blossom extract

To decorate
seasonal fruits or berries
apricot glaze (see Tip on page 94) or sifted icing sugar

To make the pastry, put the dry ingredients into a bowl and stir together. Add the butter and rub in using your fingertips until the mixture resembles breadcrumbs. Add enough of the 2–3 tablespoons water and bring together to form a dough, then knead briefly until smooth. Shape into a disc, cover with clingfilm and chill in the refrigerator for at least 1 hour.

Meanwhile, make the crème pâtissière. Heat the milk in a medium saucepan. In a heatproof bowl, whisk the egg yolks, sugar and custard powder together. Pour the warm milk over the egg mixture and whisk until smooth, then pour back into the pan, bring to the boil and cook for 1 minute, stirring continuously, until very thick and glossy. Pour into a bowl, cover the surface with clingfilm and leave to cool.

Preheat the oven to 200°C (fan 180°C)/400°F/gas mark 6. Grease 6 x individual 10cm (4in) diameter or 12 x 5cm (2in) loose-bottomed tart tins.

Roll out the pastry thinly on a floured surface and use to line the tins. Prick the bases, line with baking paper and fill with baking beans or rice. Bake in the oven for 15 minutes, then remove the paper and beans and return to the oven for a further 5 minutes until golden. Leave to cool.

Whisk the vanilla paste and orange blossom extract into the cold crème pâtissière. Spoon the crème into the cooled tart cases and decorate with fresh seasonal fruits or berries. Brush with apricot glaze or simply dust with icing sugar and serve immediately.

French blueberry tart

I once spent a summer in the Lozère region of France helping on a blueberry farm – it was an incredible experience. As well as picking the sweet fruits, we made delicious blueberry syrup, jam and this classic tart.

For the pastry
85g (3oz) unsalted butter, softened, plus extra for greasing

60g (2¼oz) golden caster sugar

1 egg

200g (7oz) plain flour, plus extra for dusting

2 tsp ground cinnamon

pinch of salt

For the filling
500g (1lb 2oz) blueberries

2 tbsp crème de cassis (optional)

125g (4½oz) golden caster sugar

2 eggs

150g (5½oz) crème fraîche

First, make the pastry. In a large bowl, cream the butter and sugar together until pale and fluffy, then beat in the egg. Add the flour, cinnamon and salt, then use a knife or your hands to mix together to form a soft dough. Knead briefly until smooth, then shape into a disc, cover with clingfilm and chill in the refrigerator for at least 1 hour.

Preheat the oven to 180°C (fan 160°C)/350°F/gas mark 4. Grease a 23cm (9in) diameter, 2cm (¾in) deep fluted tart tin.

Roll out the pastry on a lightly floured surface to 6cm (2in) larger than the prepared tin and use to line the tin. Do not prick the pastry. Line with baking paper and fill with baking beans or rice. Bake in the oven for 20–25 minutes, then remove the paper and beans and return to the oven for a further 5 minutes until golden and sandy to the touch. Set aside on a baking sheet.

Reduce the oven temperature to 160°C (fan 140°C)/325°F/gas mark 3.

Put the blueberries, crème de cassis, if using, and half the sugar into a saucepan and heat until the berries start to pop. Strain most of the juices into a jug and set aside as a serving coulis. Spoon the berries into the cooked tart.

In a small bowl, combine the remaining sugar, eggs and crème fraiche, then pour over the blueberries. Slide the tart into the oven on its baking sheet and bake for 25–30 minutes, or until set and golden with a slight wobble. Leave to cool in the tin for 15 minutes before serving with the coulis.

Linzer torte

This is a classic cake from Germany; I decided to make it in a oblong tin so you get perfect slices to serve for tea. As well as using a good buttery pastry, it is important to use a very good-quality raspberry conserve that is high in fruit for the best result.

125g (4½oz) unsalted butter, softened, plus extra for greasing

125g (4½oz) golden caster sugar

1 tsp vanilla bean paste

grated zest of 1 lemon

1 large egg, beaten

250g (9oz) plain flour, plus extra for dusting

150g (5½oz) ground almonds

1 tsp baking powder

500g (1lb 2oz) good-quality raspberry conserve

beaten egg, to glaze

apricot glaze (see Tip on page 94), to decorate

In a large bowl, cream the butter and sugar together until pale and fluffy. Add the vanilla paste and lemon zest, then gradually add the egg until combined. Sift the flour, almonds and baking powder together, then fold in. Knead the dough until smooth, being careful not to overwork it. Shape into a disc, cover with clingfilm and chill in the refrigerator for 1 hour.

Lightly grease a rectangular tart tin, about 19 x 30cm (7½ x 12in). Roll out two-thirds of the pastry on a lightly floured surface to 6cm (2in) larger than the prepared tin and use to line the tin. Add any trimmings to the remaining pastry. Fill the pastry case with the raspberry conserve, then brush the edges with beaten egg.

Roll out the remaining pastry and cut long strips of pastry about 1cm (½in) thick using a fluted pastry wheel. Arrange on top of the tart in a diagonal pattern. Chill the tart in the refrigerator for 20 minutes. Meanwhile, preheat the oven to 180°C (fan 160°C)/350°F/gas mark 4.

Brush the top of the tart with beaten egg and bake in the oven for 30–35 minutes until golden. Leave to cool completely in the tin. For extra glossiness, brush the tart with apricot glaze before serving.

Salted butter caramel brownies

This delicious brownie recipe is made even more indulgent by swirling some luscious salted butter caramel through the rich batter, which stays gooey even after baking... remember, as for any brownie recipe, don't over-bake them.

200g (7oz) unsalted butter, plus extra for greasing
200g (7oz) dark chocolate (70% cocoa solids), roughly chopped
4 eggs
175g (6oz) golden caster sugar
150g (5½oz) plain flour
1–2 tbsp dark chocolate chips

For the caramel
125g (4½oz) caster sugar
125ml (4fl oz) double cream
30g (1oz) salted butter

To make the caramel, gently melt the sugar in a heavy-based saucepan over a low heat, swirling the pan to make sure it melts evenly. Do not stir, as this may cause the caramel to seize. When melted, increase the heat slightly and bubble until it turns a dark golden colour that looks a little like mahogany. Remove from the heat and pour in half the cream, stirring as it bubbles, then return to a low heat. Add the remaining cream and the butter and stir until glossy. Pour into a heatproof bowl or jar and leave to cool and thicken.

Preheat the oven to 180°C (fan 160°C)/350°F/gas mark 4. Grease a 25 x 16cm (10 x 6¼in) rectangular brownie tin and line with baking paper.

Melt the butter and chocolate together in a heatproof bowl set over a saucepan of barely simmering water, making sure the surface of the water does not touch the bowl. Leave to cool for a few minutes. In a large bowl, whisk the eggs and sugar together until pale, fluffy and smooth, then mix in the slightly cooled chocolate mixture. Sift the flour, then fold in gently.

Pour half the brownie mixture into the prepared tin and dollop over the cooled caramel, swirling a little with a fork or spoon, then pour over the remaining brownie mixture, swirling a little. Sprinkle over the chocolate chips. Bake in the oven for 20–25 minutes until firm but not overcooked – it is all about the gooeyness! Leave to cool completely in the tin, then cut into 12 squares. Store in an airtight container.

Pâtisserie

Black-bottom cheesecake squares

This is a guilty pleasure of mine… a simple, yet striking no-bake cheesecake that does not require too much work, but at the same time is very indulgent. It's very important to use good-quality cream cheese for this recipe.

350g (12oz) Oreo biscuits
125g (4½oz) unsalted butter, melted
2 tsp powdered gelatine
4 tbsp hot water

175g (6oz) white chocolate, roughly chopped
350g (12oz) cream cheese
300ml (½ pint) double cream

1 tsp vanilla bean paste
100g (3½oz) golden caster sugar

Line the base of a 23cm (9in) square springform cake tin with baking paper.

Using a knife, open up 250g (9oz) of the Oreo biscuits. Scrape the creamy filling into a large bowl and set aside. Put the biscuits into a food processor and whizz until they resemble fine breadcrumbs. Add the melted butter and mix until well combined. Using a tablespoon, press the biscuit base evenly into the prepared tin and leave to firm up in the refrigerator.

Meanwhile, put the gelatine into a small heatproof bowl, pour over the 4 tablespoons water and set aside.

Melt the chocolate in a heatproof bowl set over a saucepan of barely simmering water, making sure the surface of the water does not touch the bowl. Leave to cool for a few minutes.

Scrape the creamy filling from the remaining biscuits and add to the bowl with the other biscuit filling, then crush the remaining biscuits and set aside.

Beat the cream cheese, cream, vanilla paste, Oreo filling and sugar together in a bowl using an electric hand whisk. Stir in the gelatine mixture and the melted white chocolate, then fold in the crushed biscuits, reserving a few crumbs for decoration.

Pour the mixture on to the biscuit base, keeping a little bit back to use as decoration. Leave to set in the refrigerator for about 4 hours. Using a sharp knife dipped in hot water, cut into 12 small squares. Add a small scoop of the remaining cream mixture to the top of each square, then dust with the reserved cookie crumbs for decoration.

Red velvet cheesecake

This recipe combines the two bestsellers at Cake Boy – red velvet and cheesecake.
It does require a little bit of effort, but it is worth it, as the reward is
an amazing-looking tasty cake.

175g (6oz) butter, softened, plus extra
for greasing
150g (5½oz) golden caster sugar
2 eggs
115g (4oz) self-raising flour
40g (1½oz) plain flour
2 tbsp unsweetened cocoa powder
¼ tsp bicarbonate of soda
125ml (4fl oz) buttermilk
2 tbsp red food colouring paste
oil, for greasing

For the filling
250g (9oz) cream cheese, at room
temperature
70g (2½oz) golden caster sugar
2 tbsp lemon juice
2 tbsp warm water
1½ tsp gelatine powder
300ml (½ pint) double cream

For the frosting
250g (9oz) cream cheese, at room
temperature
60g (2¼oz) butter, softened
85g (3oz) icing sugar, sifted
¼ tsp vanilla bean paste

Preheat the oven to 180°C (fan 160°C)/350°F/gas mark 4.
Grease a 20cm (8in) diameter deep cake tin with butter and line
the base with baking paper.

In a large bowl, cream the butter and sugar together until pale
and fluffy. Beat in the eggs, one at a time, beating well after each
addition. Sift the self-raising flour, plain flour, cocoa powder and
bicarbonate of soda together, then stir the flour mixture and
buttermilk, in alternating batches, into the butter mixture. Stir
in the food colouring.

Spoon the mixture into the prepared tin and bake in the oven for
35–40 minutes, or until a skewer inserted into the centre comes
out clean. Leave to cool in the tin for 5 minutes, then turn out on
to a cooling rack to cool completely.

To make the filling, beat the cream cheese, sugar and lemon
juice together in a bowl until smooth. Put the 2 tablespoons
water into a heatproof jug and add the gelatine.

Place the jug in a saucepan and add boiling water to come
halfway up the side of the jug. Stir until the gelatine dissolves (if
it seizes, stir gently over a low heat until it dissolves). Pour into
the filling and beat until combined. Whip the cream to soft
peaks, then fold into the cream cheese mixture.

Cut the cooled cake in half horizontally and trim the top to level
it, reserving the trimmings for decoration. Brush a 20cm (8in)
diameter springform cake tin with oil. Line the base and sides
with clingfilm, allowing it to overhang the sides. Put the cake
base, cut side up, into the tin and spread with the filling.
Sandwich together with the remaining cake. Fold over the
clingfilm and leave to set in the refrigerator overnight.

To make the frosting, beat the cream cheese, butter, icing sugar
and vanilla paste together in a bowl until well combined. Turn
the cake out on to a serving plate and spread the frosting over
the top and sides. Decorate with the reserved sponge crumbs.

Makes 6 | **Preparation time:** 20 minutes, plus cooling and freezing | **Cooking time:** 10 minutes

White chocolate and raspberry domes

This is pâtisserie at its finest and your friends will gasp in wonder if you serve these Parisian creations of white chocolate and fresh raspberries. Don't be scared to push the boat out and glaze them with a gorgeous pink jam for a professional finish.

100g (3½oz) white chocolate, roughly chopped
10g (¼oz) golden caster sugar
1 egg yolk

10g (¼oz) cornflour
50ml (2fl oz) milk
1 gelatine leaf
250ml (9fl oz) whipping cream

30 raspberries
6 thin Palets Breton (see page 156)
8 tbsp apricot jam
pink food colouring

Melt the white chocolate in a heatproof bowl set over a saucepan of barely simmering water, making sure the surface of the water does not touch the bowl. Leave to cool slightly.

In a separate heatproof bowl, whisk the sugar and egg yolk until pale and fluffy, then fold in the cornflour. Heat the milk in a saucepan, then pour over the egg mixture and whisk until smooth. Pour the mixture back into the pan and cook over a medium heat for 2–3 minutes, stirring continuously, until it has thickened.

Meanwhile, soak the gelatine in cold water until softened.

Stir the custard into the melted white chocolate. Squeeze out the excess water from the gelatine and add to the warm chocolate mixture, then stir together until the gelatine has melted.

Leave to cool. Whip the cream to soft peaks, then fold into the cooled custard.

Divide the mousse among 6 individual dome silicone moulds, filling them half full. Arrange 5 raspberries over the mousse in each mould, then spoon over the remaining mousse. Place the moulds in the freezer for at least 4 hours until set solid.

Melt the apricot jam in a small saucepan, then pass through a sieve until smooth. Return the glaze to the pan and stir in the food colouring.

Turn each mould out on to a cooling rack. Pour the glaze over the frozen domes to cover – the glaze should set within 30 seconds. Using a palette knife carefully lift each on to a Palet Breton biscuit. Chill in the refrigerator until ready to serve.

Tip~ Use dome moulds that are the same diameter as your biscuits.

Peruvian chocolate and orange mousse

Peru has produced cacao for hundreds of years, and Peruvian cacao in particular goes well with citrus flavours – this was my inspiration for this dark and rich chocolate mousse that I've paired with the smooth, sweet and zesty orange curd.

150g (5½oz) dark chocolate (preferably Peruvian), roughly chopped
150ml (¼ pint) whipping cream
30g (1oz) caster sugar

2 tbsp water
3 egg yolks
orange curd (see page 138)
a few strands of orange zest, to decorate

Melt the chocolate in a heatproof bowl set over a saucepan of barely simmering water, making sure the surface of the water does not touch the bowl. Stir occasionally, then set aside. Whip the cream until it forms soft peaks and set aside.

Place the sugar and the 2 tablespoons water in a small saucepan and heat gently, stirring until the sugar has dissolved. Bring to a rolling boil and cook until it reaches the soft-ball stage (see Tip) on a sugar thermometer (115°C/240°F).

Working quickly, whisk the egg yolks in a freestanding mixer at high speed, then slowly pour in the syrup. Continue whisking the mixture until it is light and fluffy. Leave to cool.

Fold in the melted chocolate and whipped cream, then spoon into a piping bag fitted with a 1cm (½in) piping nozzle. Pipe the mixture into 10 x individual wine or sherry glasses, filling them one-quarter full. Spoon over a good layer of curd, then top with more chocolate mousse. Decorate with the orange zest. Chill in the refrigerator until ready to serve.

Tip ~ If you don't have a sugar thermometer to tell if your sugar has reached soft-ball stage, place a saucer in the freezer until cold, and with a spoon place a small drop of the hot sugar mixture on to the saucer. If the mixture immediately sets and you can roll the drop into a ball, it is ready.

Lemon posset

This is an absolutely perfect palate cleanser and makes a gorgeous little treat when served in quirky vintage glasses – the passion fruit curd adds a touch of zesty exoticism. If you have any curd left over, keep it in the fridge for up to a week and use it to spread on hot buttered toast!

300ml (½ pint) double cream
100g (3½oz) golden caster sugar
juice of 2 lemons
passion fruit curd, to serve (see page 138)
a few strands of lemon zest, slightly blanched in hot water, to decorate

Put the cream and sugar into a saucepan and stir together over a medium-high heat. Bring to the boil and cook for 2–3 minutes, then stir in the lemon juice. Pour into 10 shot glasses or espresso cups and leave to set in the refrigerator.

To serve, using a teaspoon dipped in hot water, scoop the passion fruit curd on top of each posset. Serve decorated with the lemon zest strands.

Orange curd

60ml (2¼fl oz) orange juice
1 egg plus 1 egg yolk
85g (3oz) golden caster sugar
60g (2¼oz) unsalted butter, diced
juice of ½ lemon

In a nonstick pan, whisk the orange juice with the egg and egg yolk.
Place over a low heat and whisk until warm and thickened.

Add the sugar and butter and whisk until combined. Stir the mixture
over a low heat for about 20 minutes until it coats the back of the spoon.
Pass through a fine sieve and add lemon juice to sharpen the taste,
then leave to set in the refrigerator for a minimum of 1 hour.
Store in the refrigerator for up to 1 week.

Makes 150g | **Preparation time:** 10 minutes, plus chilling
Cooking time: 20 minutes

Passion fruit curd

6 ripe passion fruit
1 egg plus 1 egg yolk
85g (3oz) golden caster sugar
60g (2¼oz) unsalted butter, diced

Squeeze the pulp of the passion fruit into a sieve over a nonstick pan
to extract the juice. Discard the seeds. Add the egg and egg yolk. Place
the pan over a low heat and whisk until warm and thickened.

Add the sugar and butter and whisk until combined. Stir the mixture
over a low heat for about 20 minutes until it coats the back of the spoon.
Pass through a fine sieve, then leave to set in the refrigerator for a
minimum of 1 hour. Store in the refrigerator for up to 1 week.

Saffron crème pâtissière, mango and mint cups

This Indian inspired recipe combines fresh mango and mint layered with a rich saffron crème pâtissière and a thick layer of crushed cardamom biscuits for texture – yum!

200ml (7fl oz) milk
100g (3½oz) golden caster sugar
a few saffron threads
6 egg yolks
40g (1½oz) custard powder
2 ripe mangoes, peeled, stoned and cut into 3mm (⅛in) cubes
2 tbsp finely chopped mint
2 tsp vanilla bean paste
6 Cardamom Biscuits (see page 159), crushed

Put the milk, half the sugar and the saffron in a large saucepan and bring to the boil. In a large heatproof bowl, whisk the remaining sugar and egg yolks together until pale and fluffy, then add the custard powder.

Pour one-quarter of the hot milk over the yolk mixture and whisk well, then add the mixture to the milk in the pan, bring back to the boil and cook for 1 minute, stirring continuously, until very thick. Pass through a sieve into a clean bowl, cover the surface with clingfilm and chill in the refrigerator until completely cold.

When ready to serve, put the mango and mint in a bowl and toss together. Whisk the vanilla bean paste into the cold crème pâtissière. Divide the mango salsa among 6–8 small jars or teacups, filling them one-quarter full. Spoon over the crème pâtissière, then top with the crushed biscuits. Chill in the refrigerator until ready to serve.

Persian syllabub

This delicate apricot compote with sweet cinnamon is topped with the lightest of creamy concoctions… it's as if little clouds have landed in these beautiful glasses!

400ml (14fl oz) double cream
4 tbsp golden caster sugar
1 tbsp lemon juice
2 tbsp apricot brandy
1 tsp rose extract
edible dried rose petals, to serve

For the compote
400g (14oz) ripe apricots, halved and stoned
50ml (2fl oz) water
50g (1¾oz) golden caster sugar
¼ tsp ground cinnamon, plus extra for dusting

First, make the compote. Put the apricots, the 50ml (2fl oz) water, the sugar and cinnamon in a heavy-based saucepan and cook over a low heat for about 5 minutes, or until the fruits have softened but still retain their shape. Spoon into a bowl and leave to cool.

Using a balloon whisk, whip the cream, sugar, lemon juice, brandy and rose extract together to soft peaks, being careful not to over-whisk – the mixture should just hold its shape (this will happen very quickly because of the alcohol and lemon juice).

Divide the compote among 6 x individual 175ml (6fl oz) tea glasses, then spoon over swirls of the cream mixture. Leave to set in the refrigerator for at least 4 hours.

To serve, dust with cinnamon and sprinkle with edible rose petals.

Tip ~ If fresh apricots are out of season, substitute canned apricots.

Kheer

I like my afternoon teas to be entertaining until the very last bite and that's why I like to include an unusual dish or flavours for my guests to talk about. This fragrant Indian rice pudding is extraordinarily flavoursome and looks really pretty served in mini tagine dishes.

600ml (20fl oz) milk
70g (2½oz) golden caster sugar
6 whole green cardamom pods, lightly crushed
25g (1oz) unsalted butter
50g (1¾oz) carnaroli risotto rice
100ml (3½fl oz) orange juice
1 tsp orange blossom extract
1 tsp rose extract
1 tsp vanilla bean paste

To serve
25g (1oz) shelled pistachio nuts, roasted and roughly chopped (see Tip on page 17)
edible dried rose petals

Put the milk, sugar and cardamom pods into a small saucepan and heat gently to simmering point. Remove from the heat and leave to infuse.

Meanwhile, melt the butter in a medium-sized saucepan and stir in the rice. Mix well to coat the grains in the butter, then add the orange juice. Bring to the boil, then reduce the heat and simmer for 2–3 minutes.

Remove the cardamom pods from the milk, pour the milk on to the rice and cook gently for about 30 minutes until the mixture has thickened and the rice is tender.

Stir in the orange blossom and rose extracts and vanilla paste, then spoon into 10 small bowls. Sprinkle with the chopped pistachios and rose petals and serve warm.

LEFT Coffee and hazelnut meringues
RIGHT Iles flottantes

Coffee and hazelnut meringues

Meringues are so much fun to make… you can flavour them with so many ingredients, tint them the colours of the rainbow… the sky's the limit! These are simply flavoured with coffee extract and baked with a hazelnut praline… and, of course, served with a whipped vanilla cream.

oil, for greasing
4 egg whites
225g (8oz) golden icing sugar
2 tsp coffee extract

250ml (9fl oz) whipping cream
1 tsp vanilla bean paste
grated dark chocolate, to decorate

For the hazelnut praline
100g (3½oz) caster sugar
100g (3½oz) blanched hazelnuts, roasted (see Tip on page 17)

Preheat the oven to 120°C (fan 100°C)/250°F/gas mark ½. Lightly grease a baking sheet with oil and line a second baking sheet with baking paper.

First, make the praline. Gently melt the sugar in a heavy-based saucepan over a low heat, swirling the pan to make sure it melts evenly. Do not stir, as this may cause it to seize. When melted, increase the heat slightly and bubble until it turns an amber colour. Stir in the nuts, then pour on to the oiled baking sheet and leave to cool.

In a large, clean, dry bowl, whisk the egg whites to soft peaks. Whisk in half the icing sugar, 1 tablespoon at a time, until the mixture is stiff and glossy. Carefully fold in the remaining sugar, followed by the coffee extract.

Spread the mixture into 12 circles, 6cm (2½in) in diameter, on the lined baking sheet. Break the praline up into small pieces and scatter most of it over the meringues, reserving some for decoration.

Bake in the oven for 1½–2 hours until the meringues are dry and lift easily from the paper. Leave to cool completely.

Whip the cream and vanilla paste together to soft peaks. Spoon on to the cool meringues and scatter over the reserved praline. Sprinkle with grated chocolate and serve immediately.

Makes 8 | **Preparation time:** 15 minutes, plus cooling | **Cooking time:** 20 minutes

Îles flottantes

When I was a kid it was always an exciting day when my mum made îles flottantes, and I have fond memories of her poaching the soft meringue in simmering water. These are a mini version of my childhood recipe and I have given the custard a caramel flavour for a more grown-up taste.

For the custard
350ml (12fl oz) milk
70g (2½oz) golden caster sugar
3 egg yolks
2 tsp vanilla bean paste

For the meringues
3 egg whites
pinch of salt
125g (4½oz) caster sugar

To decorate
blanched almonds, roughly chopped

First, make the custard. Heat the milk in a saucepan until warm and set aside. Meanwhile, gently melt the sugar in a medium heavy-based saucepan over a low heat, swirling the pan to make sure it melts evenly. Do not stir, as this may cause it to seize. When melted, increase the heat slightly and bubble until it turns an amber colour. Add the warm milk, stirring until the caramel has dissolved.

Put the egg yolks into a bowl, pour over a little of the caramel milk and whisk together, then pour the mixture back into the pan and cook gently, stirring continuously, until the custard coats the back of a wooden spoon. Pass through a sieve into a clean bowl. Cover the surface with clingfilm and leave to cool. When cold, stir in the vanilla bean paste.

To make the meringues, bring a large saucepan of water to the boil. In a clean, dry bowl, whisk the egg whites and a pinch of salt to stiff peaks, then add the sugar, a little at a time, whisking continuously until it is thick and glossy.

Using a small ice cream scoop dipped into hot water, scoop perfect balls of meringue and place them on the simmering water. Cook for 30 seconds on each side, then lift gently on to kitchen paper to drain. Repeat with the remaining mixture to make 8 meringues.

Spoon the cooled caramel custard into 8 x 300ml (½ pint) teacups, filling them about half full, then gently top each with a meringue. Chill in the refrigerator until ready to serve, then scatter with blanched almonds just before serving.

Chocolate ganache hearts

Most people like chocolate and you can't go wrong with a beautifully moist chocolate sponge coated with a rich glossy ganache... and it's even more difficult to resist if it is heart-shaped.

For the sponge
butter, for greasing
1 large egg
200g (7oz) golden caster sugar
175g (6oz) Greek yogurt
75ml (2½fl oz) vegetable oil

2 tsp vanilla bean paste
3 tbsp espresso coffee
70g (2½oz) unsweetened cocoa powder
125g (4½oz) plain flour
½ tsp baking powder
pinch of salt

For the chocolate ganache
300g (10½oz) dark chocolate, 70% cocoa solids, roughly chopped
150ml (¼ pint) double cream
1 tsp vanilla extract

First, make the sponge. Preheat the oven to 170°C (fan 140°C)/325°F/gas mark 3. Grease 4 x individual 7cm (2¾in) wide heart-shaped cake tins.

In a large bowl, whisk the egg, sugar, yogurt, oil and vanilla together until smooth and combined. Add the coffee and cocoa powder and whisk vigorously until the mixture is smooth and free from lumps. Sift the flour, baking powder and salt together, then add to the mixture and whisk vigorously for about 1 minute until just combined.

Pour the mixture into the prepared tins and bake in the oven for about 25 minutes, or until a skewer inserted into the centre comes out clean. Leave to cool in the tins for 10 minutes, then carefully turn out on to a cooling rack and leave to cool completely.

To make the ganache, melt the chocolate in a heatproof bowl set over a saucepan of barely simmering water, making sure the surface of the water does not touch the bowl. Meanwhile, put the cream into a saucepan and heat to just below boiling point.

Remove the melted chocolate from the heat and slowly pour in the cream, gently stirring with a balloon whisk until smooth and glossy. Add the vanilla extract and stir to combine. Leave to stand for about 10 minutes until cool and slightly thickened.

Stand the cakes on a wire rack over a baking sheet. Beat the ganache briefly before pouring it over the cakes. Lightly smooth and spread the ganache over the top and sides of the cakes with a palette knife. Leave to stand at room temperature until set before serving.

Tip ~ If you don't have individual heart-shaped tins, bake the mixture in a 20 x 20cm (8 x 8in) square cake tin at 170°C (fan 140°C)/325°F/gas mark 3 for 25 minutes, or until a skewer inserted into the centre comes out clean. Leave to cool in the tin for 10 minutes, then carefully turn out on to a cooling rack and cut into squares.

Raspberry choux craquelin buns

Who would have thought that adding a fine layer of flavoured shortcrust pastry on top of unbaked choux pastry would have such a great result? The combination gives a light fluffy choux with a crunchy ruby-red top… which goes perfectly with cream and fresh raspberries.

For the craquelin
25g (1oz) unsalted butter, softened

30g (1oz) light muscovado sugar

30g (1oz) plain flour

2 drops of pink food colouring

2 drops of raspberry extract

For the choux buns
40g (1½oz) unsalted butter, cut into small cubes

¼ tsp salt

½ tsp golden caster sugar

75ml (2½fl oz) milk

50ml (2fl oz) water

70g (2½oz) plain flour

3 eggs

For the filling
300ml (½ pint) whipping cream

1 tsp vanilla extract

500g (1lb 2oz) fresh raspberries

First, make the craquelin. In a large bowl, beat together all the ingredients until smooth. Turn the mixture out on to a sheet of baking paper, cover with a second sheet and roll out to 2mm (¹⁄₁₆in) thick. Freeze for 2 hours until set.

Preheat the oven to 180°C (fan 160°C)/350°F/gas mark 4. Line a baking sheet with baking paper.

Put the butter, salt, sugar, milk and the 50ml (2fl oz) water into a saucepan and heat gently until the butter is melted, then bring to the boil. Tip in the flour and beat the mixture over a medium heat using a wooden spoon until the ingredients bind together to form a dough. Turn the dough into a bowl and leave to cool for 2–3 minutes, then beat in the eggs one at the time.

Tip the choux paste into a piping bag fitted with a 2cm (1in) diameter plain piping nozzle. Pipe 10 x 6cm (2½in) diameter buns on to the prepared baking sheet. Using a 6cm (2½in) diameter plain cookie cutter, stamp out 10 discs from the frozen craquelin, then gently lay over the choux buns.

Bake in the oven for 20–25 minutes until golden and dry, briefly opening the door after 10 minutes to let out the steam. Pierce the bases to release the steam. Transfer to a cooling rack to cool completely.

When cold, cut the buns in half. Whip the cream and vanilla extract together, then spoon into a piping bag fitted with a 1cm (½in) diameter star piping nozzle. Pipe the cream into the bun bases, then arrange the raspberries over the cream. Top with the bun lids and serve.

Makes 10 | **Preparation time:** 20 minutes, plus cooling | **Cooking time:** 25 minutes

Cranberry and white chocolate whoopie pies

I think whoopie pies are fun and a great way to use up any leftover sponge batter. This recipe has a festive feel with cranberries and the addition of orange, but for me the traditional indulgent marshmallow filling really make these cuties special.

1 large egg
150g (5½oz) light muscovado sugar
70g (2½oz) unsalted butter, melted
125ml (4fl oz) soured cream
2 tbsp milk
½ tsp vanilla bean paste
2–3 drops of orange blossom extract
250g (9oz) plain flour
3 tsp bicarbonate of soda
50g (1¾oz) sun-dried cranberries

For the marshmallow cream
50g (1¾oz) white chocolate, roughly chopped
100g (3½oz) white marshmallows
50ml (2fl oz) milk
2–3 drops of vanilla bean paste
125g (4½oz) very soft unsalted butter

For the topping
100g (3½oz) white chocolate, roughly chopped
50g (1¾oz) white chocolate curls

Preheat the oven to 180°C (fan 160°C)/350°F/gas mark 4. Line a large baking sheet with baking paper.

In a large bowl, whisk the egg and beat in the sugar one-third at a time. In a separate bowl, mix the melted butter, soured cream, milk, vanilla paste and orange extract together, then stir into the egg and sugar mixture. Sift in the flour and bicarbonate of soda and beat until smooth. Gently fold in the cranberries.

Tip the mixture into a piping bag fitted with a 2cm (1in) diameter plain piping nozzle. Pipe 20 large walnut-sized balls on to the prepared baking sheet. Bake in the oven for 13–14 minutes until spongy and golden around the edges. Transfer to a cooling rack to cool completely.

To make the marshmallow cream, melt the white chocolate in a heatproof bowl set over a saucepan of barely simmering water, making sure the surface of the water does not touch the bowl. Put the marshmallows and milk in a saucepan and cook over a low heat, stirring until smooth. Stir in the melted white chocolate and leave to cool. Beat the butter in a bowl until creamy and soft, then gradually beat in the marshmallow mixture until smooth.

Melt the remaining white chocolate as above and leave to cool slightly. Spread the marshmallow cream over the flat side of half the whoopie cakes or pipe it on for a neater appearance. Sandwich together with the remaining cakes. Top each with the melted white chocolate and sprinkle over the white chocolate curls.

Biscuits

Viennese butter biscuits

These delicate and super-buttery classic biscuits are perfect for an elegant and sophisticated afternoon tea. Dipping them in dark chocolate makes them even more difficult to resist.

100g (3½oz) unsalted butter, softened, plus extra for greasing

25g (1oz) icing sugar

1 tsp vanilla bean paste

100g (3½oz) plain flour

1 tsp cornflour

¼ tsp baking powder

1–2 tsp milk

50g (1¾oz) milk chocolate, roughly chopped

50g (1¾oz) dark chocolate (70% cocoa solids), roughly chopped

Preheat the oven to 170°C (fan 140°C)/325°F/gas mark 3. Lightly grease a baking sheet.

In a large bowl, cream the butter and sugar together until pale and fluffy. Add the vanilla paste and beat again. Sift the flour, cornflour and baking powder together, then fold in until thoroughly combined and the mixture is smooth. Add the milk to loosen slightly.

Spoon the mixture into a piping bag fitted with a medium star-shaped piping nozzle, then pipe fingers, 10cm (4in) long, on to the prepared sheet. Bake on the middle shelf of the oven for 10–15 minutes until pale golden. Leave to cool on the sheet for 5 minutes, then transfer to a cooling rack to cool completely.

Melt the chocolates together in a heatproof bowl set over a saucepan of barely simmering water, making sure the surface of the water does not touch the bowl. Pour into the smallest bowl that you have (this will make it easier to dip), then very gently dip one end of each cooled Viennese biscuit into the chocolate. Leave to set on a baking sheet lined with baking paper. Store in an airtight container.

Palets Breton

I grew up eating these buttery shortbreads almost on a daily basis – they simply melt in your mouth. This traditional biscuit from my native Brittany can also be used as a base for other recipes too (see page 132).

2 egg yolks
85g (3oz) golden caster sugar
85g (3oz) unsalted butter, softened
140g (5oz) plain flour, plus extra for dusting
1 tsp baking powder
2 generous pinches of Guérande salt

In a bowl, whisk together the egg yolks and sugar until pale and fluffy, then add the butter. Sift the flour, baking powder and salt together, then add to the mixture and combine together to form a smooth dough.

Turn out on to a lightly floured surface and shape into a 3cm (1¼in) diameter sausage. Cover with clingfilm and chill in the refrigerator for at least 2 hours.

Preheat the oven to 180°C (fan 160°C)/350°F/gas mark 4. Line a thin baking sheet with baking paper.

Slice the dough into 15mm (⅝in) thick rounds for chunky biscuits (as in the photograph opposite) or 8mm (⅜in) thick rounds for thinner biscuits and place on the prepared baking sheet. Bake in the oven for 20 minutes until golden with slightly darker edges. Leave to cool completely on the sheet. Store in an airtight container.

Tip~ To help keep the shape of the biscuits, put the dough rounds inside chef's cooking rings or in the holes of a cupcake tin before baking.

Cardamom biscuits

These little square biscuits are packed with butter, cardamom and golden caster sugar and have a very exotic flavour that is perfect with a strong tea… I just love the crunch from the sugar-dipped corners!

300g (10½oz) plain flour, plus extra for dusting
125g (4½oz) golden caster sugar, plus extra to decorate
½ tsp cardamom powder
200g (7oz) cold unsalted butter, diced, plus extra for greasing
2 tsp vanilla bean paste
about 25 whole blanched almonds

Put the flour, sugar and cardamom in a large bowl and mix together. Add the butter and rub in using your fingertips until the mixture resembles breadcrumbs. Add the vanilla paste and knead briefly to form a dough, being careful not to overwork it. Shape into a disc, cover with clingfilm and chill in the refrigerator for 1 hour.

Grease a large baking sheet. Roll out the dough on a floured surface to 1cm (½in) thick. Stamp out biscuits using a cookie cutter of your choice, then place on the prepared sheet and push an almond into each. Place the sheet in the refrigerator for 20 minutes. Meanwhile, preheat the oven to 170°C (fan 140°C)/325°F/gas mark 3.

Bake in the oven for 12 minutes until golden around the edges. Leave to cool slightly on the sheet, then dip into golden caster sugar and transfer to a cooling rack to cool completely. Store in an airtight container.

Makes 24 | **Preparation time:** 15 minutes | **Cooking time:** 10–12 minutes

Soft ginger biscuits

Gorgeous and chewy, these little treats are a mixture between a cookie and a cake – they are lovely and light too.

125g (4½oz) unsalted butter, softened, plus extra for greasing
275g (9¾oz) plain flour
1 tbsp ground ginger
1 tsp bicarbonate of soda
¾ tsp ground cinnamon
¼ tsp ground cloves
200g (7oz) golden caster sugar, plus extra for sprinkling
1 egg
1 tbsp water
4 tbsp black treacle

Preheat the oven to 180°C (fan 160°C)/350°F/gas mark 4. Lightly grease 2 baking sheets.

Sift the flour, ginger, bicarbonate of soda, cinnamon and cloves together into a large bowl. In a separate bowl, cream the butter and sugar together until pale and fluffy. Beat in the egg, then stir in the 1 tablespoon water and the treacle. Gradually fold in the dry ingredients to form a dough.

Shape the dough into walnut-sized balls and place 5cm (2in) apart on the prepared baking sheets, then flatten slightly and sprinkle with sugar.

Bake in the oven for 10–12 minutes until just turning golden. Leave to cool on the sheets for 5 minutes, then transfer to a cooling rack to cool completely. Store in an airtight container.

Makes 12 | **Preparation time:** 15 minutes, plus chilling | **Cooking time:** 15 minutes

Honey and lemon biscuits

Anything with lemon in always gets my thumbs up… the zesty flavour in these biscuits is tamed by the sweet honey. A sweet herbal tea such as lemon verbena would be a perfect accompaniment.

175g (6oz) plain flour
1 tsp baking powder
1 egg, beaten
grated zest of 2 lemons
50ml (2fl oz) lemon juice
85g (3oz) clear honey
2 tbsp olive oil, plus extra for greasing
icing sugar, for dusting

Sift the flour and baking powder together into a large bowl, then add the egg, lemon zest and juice, honey and olive oil and mix together until smooth. Cover with clingfilm and chill in the refrigerator for 30 minutes.

Preheat the oven to 180°C (fan 160°C)/350°F/gas mark 4. Grease a large baking sheet and line with baking paper.

Spoon the mixture into a piping bag fitted with a 1cm (½in) diameter plain piping nozzle, then pipe 4cm (1½in) diameter rounds on to the prepared baking sheet. Dust with icing sugar.

Bake in the oven for 15 minutes, or until the edges are golden. Transfer to a cooling rack to cool completely. Dust with extra icing sugar before serving. Store carefully in an airtight container.

Lavender shortbread hearts

What I like most about baking with lavender is how you can use the natural dried flowers to perfume your shortbread instead of using oil or extract, which gives the finished product a subtle scent and, of course, looks very pretty too. These heart-shaped shortbreads are perfect for a Valentine's Day tea.

175g (6oz) unsalted butter, softened
70g (2½oz) caster sugar
2 tbsp icing sugar, sifted
1½ tsp finely chopped culinary dried lavender
225g (8oz) plain flour, plus extra for dusting
50g (1¾oz) cornflour
pinch of salt

In a medium bowl, cream the butter, caster sugar and icing sugar together until pale and fluffy, then mix in the lavender. Sift the flour, cornflour and salt together, then fold in until well blended.

Flatten the dough to about 2.5cm (1in) thick and cover with clingfilm. Chill in the refrigerator for about 1 hour until firm.

Preheat the oven to 170°C (fan 140°C)/325°F/gas mark 3. Line 2 baking sheets with baking paper.

Roll out the dough on a floured surface to 5mm (¼in) thick. Using a heart-shaped cookie cutter, stamp out 24 shapes, re-rolling the trimmings as necessary, then transfer to the prepared baking sheets.

Bake in the oven for 18–20 minutes until the shortbread starts to brown at the edges. Leave to cool for a few minutes on the sheets, then transfer to a cooling rack to cool completely. Store in an airtight container.

Makes 30 | **Preparation time:** 20 minutes, plus cooling and setting | **Cooking time:** about 50 minutes

Cranberry and pistachio biscotti

These cute little biscotti are crunchy and yummy, and make a very colourful addition to your table. They are perfect served with an Italian coffee or hot chocolate.

90g (3¼oz) unsalted butter, softened
100g (3½oz) golden caster sugar
2 large eggs
1 tbsp grated lemon zest
1½ tsp vanilla bean paste
300g (10½oz) plain flour, plus extra for dusting
1½ tsp baking powder
115g (4oz) dried cranberries
100g (3½oz) shelled pistachio nuts
200g (7oz) white chocolate, roughly chopped

Preheat the oven to 180°C (fan 160°C)/350°F/gas mark 4. Line 2 large baking sheets with baking paper.

In a large bowl, cream the butter and sugar together until pale and fluffy. Beat in the eggs one at a time, then fold in the lemon zest and vanilla paste. Sift the flour and baking powder together and fold in. Add the cranberries and pistachios and mix to form a dough.

Turn the dough out on to a lightly floured surface and divide in half. Shape each into a log about 3cm (1¼in) wide. Carefully transfer to one of the prepared baking sheets, spacing the logs 10cm (4in) apart. Bake in the oven for about 30 minutes until almost firm to touch but still pale. Leave to cool on the sheets for 10 minutes.

Carefully transfer the logs to a chopping board. Using a serrated knife and a gentle sawing motion, cut the logs crossways into generous 1cm (½in) thick slices. Place the slices on the baking sheets, return to the oven and bake for a further 18 minutes until firm and pale golden, turning the slices over halfway through the cooking time. Transfer to a cooling rack to cool completely.

Melt the white chocolate in a heatproof bowl set over a saucepan of barely simmering water, making sure the surface of the water does not touch the bowl. Drizzle each cooled biscotti with melted chocolate, then leave to set on a baking sheet lined with baking paper. Store in an airtight container.

Makes 16–18 | **Preparation time:** 15 minutes, plus chilling, cooling and setting | **Cooking time:** about 15 minutes

Peanut butter and banana cookies

A combination made in heaven in biscuit form: ripe banana and, importantly, crunchy peanut butter for extra va-va-voom!

125g (4½oz) mashed ripe banana
100g (3½oz) crunchy peanut butter
70g (2½oz) butter, melted
50g (1¾oz) dark muscovado sugar
85g (3oz) golden caster sugar
1 tsp vanilla bean paste
200g (7oz) self-raising flour
2 tsp baking powder
40g (1½oz) dark chocolate chips
100g (3½oz) dark chocolate, roughly chopped

In a bowl, mix the banana, peanut butter and melted butter together until blended. Stir in the muscovado sugar, caster sugar and vanilla paste until smooth. Sift the flour and baking powder, then fold into the peanut butter mixture to form a dough. Mix in the chocolate chips. Cover with clingfilm and chill in the refrigerator for at least 1 hour.

Preheat the oven to 180°C (fan 160°C)/350°F/gas mark 4. Line a baking sheet with baking paper.

Using a dessertspoon, scoop out spoonfuls of the dough and place on the prepared baking sheet. Flatten each with the palm of your hand. Bake in the oven for 10–12 minutes until golden and slightly risen. Leave to cool on the sheet for 5 minutes, then transfer to a cooling rack to cool completely.

Melt the chocolate in a heatproof bowl set over a saucepan of barely simmering water, making sure the surface of the water does not touch the bowl. Drizzle the cooled cookies with the melted chocolate and leave to set on a baking sheet lined with baking paper. Store in an airtight container.

Coconut macarons rocher

This was the first recipe I ever baked, when I was just five years old. These little coconut mounds are very easy to make, which makes them a perfect recipe for the kids to get involved in. It's an added bonus that they taste really good, too.

4 rice/wafer paper sheets
175g (6oz) golden caster sugar
250g (9oz) desiccated coconut
3 egg whites

Preheat the oven to 180°C (fan 160°C)/350°F/gas mark 4. Line a baking sheet with rice/wafer paper.

Put the sugar and coconut in a bowl and mix together. In a separate clean, dry bowl, whisk the egg whites to soft peaks, then fold in the coconut mixture. Dollop spoonfuls of the mixture on to the wafer paper, building each into a pyramid shape with your fingers and the back of a spoon.

Bake in the oven for 15 minutes until golden. Leave to cool on the baking sheet for 5 minutes, then transfer to a cooling rack to cool completely. Break the excess rice/wafer paper away from the base of the macarons. Store in an airtight container.

Tip ~ For more indulgence, drizzle over or dip the bases into melted dark chocolate.

Gluten-free tahini cookies

I discovered tahini after visiting Turkey, where this ingredient is used a lot in both savoury and sweet baking. The addition of the ground almonds, honey and olive oil gives these cookies a real flavour of the Middle East.

140g (5oz) ground almonds
1 tsp baking powder
150g (5½oz) clear honey
100g (3½oz) tahini
1 tbsp olive oil
½ tsp vanilla bean paste
16 whole blanched almonds
golden icing sugar, for dusting

Preheat the oven to 180°C (fan 160°C)/350°F/gas mark 4. Line 2 baking sheets with baking paper.

In a large bowl, mix the ground almonds and baking powder together. Put the honey, tahini, oil and vanilla paste into a jug and stir together. Pour the wet ingredients into the dry and stir well, then using your hands, bring together to form a ball of dough. (The dough should be fairly stiff – if it is too soft, add a few more ground almonds.)

Divide the dough into 16 pieces and shape into balls, then transfer to the prepared baking sheets. Flatten with a fork, then press an almond into the centre of each.

Bake in the oven for 10–12 minutes until golden. Transfer to a cooling rack and leave to cool. Dust lightly with sugar before serving. Store in an airtight container for up to 1 week.

Cinnamon palmiers

I don't think we see enough palmiers around. When made properly, this French classic is simply gorgeous, what with all the lovely caramelization that takes place during baking. I simply add a little ground cinnamon to give this legendary biscuit my own little twist.

4 tbsp golden caster sugar
1 tbsp ground cinnamon
375g (13oz) ready-rolled sheet all-butter puff pastry

Preheat the oven to 200°C (fan 180°C)/400°F/gas mark 6. Line a baking sheet with baking paper.

Put the sugar and cinnamon into a bowl and mix together. Unroll the pastry sheet and sprinkle half the cinnamon sugar over the top. Using a rolling pin, roll the pastry to press in the sugar. Turn the pastry over and repeat.

Starting at the shorter edge, fold over 2cm (¾in) of the pastry towards the centre. Continue folding the pastry over until you reach the centre. Do the same on the other side of the pastry so that the folded sides meet in the centre, then fold them over each other. Slice into 1cm (½in) thick slices, then place them flat on the prepared baking sheet, about 2cm (¾in) apart. Chill in the refrigerator for 15 minutes.
Bake in the oven for 10–12 minutes, or until golden brown. Serve warm or cold.

Index

A

al fresco summer picnic 11
almonds, ground
    carrot & coconut cake 86
    chocolate cake 90
    clementine & pomegranate cake 103
    fresh fig cake 106
    in Linzer torte 122
    in macarons 14–21
    pistachio & rose financiers 89
    tahini cookies 170
Aperol sultana scones 78–9
apple
    & Camembert tarts with walnut drizzle 44–5
    Scandinavian apple cake 94–5
apricot
    candied apricot cake 98–9
    glaze for cakes 94
    in Persian syllabub 140
Arabian dream menu 10
asparagus, pickled vegetable bundles 66
Autumn comfort menu 11

B

banana
    & peanut butter cookies 166–7
    & walnut bundt cake 84–5
bee pollen & orange blossom scones 69
beef, cacao beef on pain perdu 64–5
beetroot
    & caraway bread with vanilla-cured salmon 56–7
    & coriander macarons 18–19, 20
berries
    tartelettes aux fruits 118–19
    see also types of berries
biscuits & cookies
    cardamom biscuits 139, 158–9
    cinnamon palmiers 171
    cranberry & pistachio biscotti 164–5
    gluten-free tahini cookies 170

    honey & lemon biscuits 162
    lavender shortbread hearts 163
    Oreo 128
    Palets Breton 156–7
    peanut butter & banana cookies 166–7
    soft ginger biscuits 160–1
    Viennese butter biscuits 154–5
black tea 8
    vanilla flavoured 10
blue cheese
    gougères 26, 28
    pear & walnut tartlets 37
blueberries
    French blueberry tart 120–1
    tartelettes aux fruits 118
Brie & red onion éclairs 23, 25
brioche
    cacao beef on pain perdu 64–5
    roast beef, watercress & horseradish buns 51, 53
brownies, salted butter caramel 124–5
bundt cake
    spiced banana & walnut 84–5
    triple marble 108–9
buttermilk, in scones 68–79

C

cacao
    beef on pain perdu 65
    & raspberry scones 74–5
    see also chocolate
cake
    black-bottom cheesecake 128–9
    candied apricot cake 98–9
    carrot & coconut cake, gluten- & sugar-free 86–7
    chocolate, gluten-free 90–1
    chocolate ganache hearts 146–7
    chocolate & ginger tart 115
    clementine & pomegranate 102–3
    coffee & walnut 100–1
    French flourless cake 105

    fresh fig cake 106–7
    light Italian fruit cake 104
    matcha & lemon 114, 116
    orange & cranberry nutty tea loaf 93
    orange marmalade squares 92
    pistachio & rose financiers 88–9
    red velvet cheesecake 130–1
    salted butter caramel brownies 124–5
    Scandinavian apple cake 94–5
    spiced banana & walnut bundt cake 84–5
    sticky pecan cake 110–11
    strawberry ombre cake 112–13
    triple marble bundt cake 108–9
    upside down pineapple cakes 96–7
Camembert & apple tarts with walnut drizzle 44–5
caramel
    custard 145
    salted butter 124
cardamom biscuits 139, 158–9
carrot
    & coconut cake, gluten- & sugar-free 86–7
    pickled vegetable bundles 66
Celebration menu 11
Ceylon tea 8
Cheddar cheese
    gougères 28
    scones 81
cheese
    scones 81
    see also types of cheese
cheesecake
    black-bottom no-bake 128–9
    red velvet 130–1
chicken
    paprika chicken ciabattas 62
chocolate
    black-bottom cheesecake 128–9
    cake, gluten-free 90–1
    cranberry & pistachio biscotti 164–5

cranberry & white chocolate whoopie pies
    150–1
French flourless cake 105
ganache hearts 146–7
& ginger tart 115, 117
matcha & lemon cake 116
peanut butter & banana cookies 166–7
Peruvian chocolate & orange mousse 134–5
red velvet cheesecake 130–1
salted butter caramel brownies 124–5
triple marble bundt cake 108–9
Viennese butter biscuits 154–5
white chocolate & raspberry domes
    132–3
choux pastry 36
    éclairs 22–5
    gougères 26, 28
    mini Paris-Brest 30–1
    profiteroles 27, 29
    raspberry craquelin buns 148–9
ciabatta, paprika chicken 62
cinnamon palmiers 171
clementine & pomegranate cake 102–3
coconut
    & carrot cake, gluten- & sugar-free 86–7
    in chocolate cake 90
    macarons rocher 168–9
    upside down pineapple cakes 96–7
coffee
    chocolate ganache hearts 147
    & hazelnut meringues 142, 144
    & walnut cake 100–1
compote, apricot 140
cookies see biscuits & cookies
coriander & beetroom macarons 18–19, 20
crab, curried crab filo tartlets 38, 40
cranberry
    & orange nutty tea loaf 93
    & pistachio biscotti 164–5
    & white chocolate whoopie pies 150–1
craquelin, raspberry choux buns 148–9

cream cheese
    black-bottom cheesecake 128–9
    frosting 84, 112
    lemon & pepper macarons with smoked salmon
        14
    red velvet cheesecake 130–1
crème pâtissière 118
    saffron 139
cucumber, pickled vegetable bundles 66
curd
    lemon posset 137
    orange 138
    passion fruit 138
custard
    crème pâtissière 118, 139
    Iles flottantes 143, 145

D
Darjeeling tea 8
dolcelatte cheese & walnut macarons 17
dried fruit, light Italian fruit cake 104

E
Earl Grey tea 10
éclairs
    Brie & red onion 23, 25
    porcini & pancetta 22, 24
egg Florentine roulade 54–5

F
fennel 63
fig
    fresh fig cake 106–7
    & Parma ham macarons 19, 21
filo pastry, curried crab tartlets 38, 40
financiers, pistachio & rose 88–9
focaccia, spinach, with salmon & keta tartare 50, 52
French flourless cake 105
frosting
    cream cheese 84, 112, 130
    mascarpone & coffee 100

fruit
    glacé 77, 97, 104
    light Italian fruit cake 104
    tartelettes 118–19
    teas 8, 9, 10

G
ganache
    chocolate 90
    chocolate hearts 146–7
ginger
    biscuits 160–1
    & chocolate tart 115, 117
gluten-free recipes
    carrot & coconut cake 86–7
    chocolate cake 90–1
    clementine & pomegranate cake 102–3
    tahini cookies 170
gougères, blue cheese 26, 28
green tea 8, 9, 11, 116
Gruyère cheese
    blue cheese gougères 28
    éclairs with brie & red onion 25
    scones 81

H
hazelnut
    & coffee meringues 142, 144
    macarons with pumpkin purée 16
    orange & cranberry tea loaf 93
herbal infusions 8, 9, 10
honey
    & lemon biscuits 162
    tahini cookies 170
horseradish 53

I
Iles flottantes 143, 145
Indian rice pudding 141

K

Kenyan tea 8
keta 31, 52
kheer 141

L

Lady Grey tea 11
Lapsang Souchong 8, 11
lardons, tartes flambées 41
lavender shortbread hearts 163
leeks, tartelettes de Saint Jacques 34–5
lemon
   & honey biscuits 162
   & matcha cake 114, 116
   posset 136–7
   scones 70, 72
Linzer torte 122–3
lobster, herby lobster rolls 58–9
loose tea 9

M

macarons
   beetroot & coriander 18–19, 20
   coconut macarons rocher 168–9
   hazelnut, with pumpkin purée 16
   lemon & pepper, with smoked salmon 14 15
   Parma ham & fig 19, 21
   walnut & dolcelatte 17
mango & mint cups with saffron crème pâtissière
   139
maple syrup 111
marshmallow cream 151
mascarpone cheese, Parma ham & fig macarons
   21
matcha & lemon cake 114, 116
melon, cantaloupe & Parma ham macarons 21
menus 10–11
meringues
   coffee & hazelnut 142, 144
   Iles flottantes 143, 145
Mother's Day menu 10

mousse
   Peruvian chocolate & orange 134–5
   salmon 30–1
mozzarella
   caprice profiteroles 29
   tomato & olive tarts 42–3

N

nigella seeds 21, 31

O

olive, tomato & mozzarella tarts 43
onion marmalade 25
orange
   Aperol sultana scones 78
   candied apricot cake 98
   & cranberry nutty tea loaf 93
   curd 138
   in kheer 141
   marmalade squares 92
   orange blossom & bee pollen scones 69
   & Peruvian chocolate mousse 134–5
   syrup on fresh fig cake 106

P

Palets Breton 156–7
palmiers, cinnamon 171
pancetta & porcini éclairs 22, 24
panettone scones 76–7
Paris-Brest, salmon mousse & nigella seed 30–1
Parma ham & fig macarons 19, 21
Parmesan cheese, spinach & pine nut wholemeal
tartlets 47
passion fruit curd 138
pastry
   choux 36
   with ground almonds 122
   puff 44, 171
   shortcrust 36, 47, 118
peanut butter & banana cookies 166–7
pear, Roquefort & walnut tartlets 37

pecan nuts
   carrot & coconut cake 86
   sticky pecan cake 110–11
Persian syllabub 140
Peruvian chocolate & orange mousse 134–5
pickled vegetable bundles 66
picnic menu 11
pine nut & spinach wholemeal tartlets 46–7
pineapple upside down mini cakes 96–7
pistachio
   candied apricot cake 98
   & cranberry biscotti 164–5
   & rose financiers 88–9
   & rose scones 71, 73
pomegranate & clementine cake 102–3
porcini & pancetta éclairs 22, 24
praline, hazelnut 144
prawns, tequila king prawn sliders 60–1
profiteroles, caprice 27
puff pastry
   cinnamon palmiers 171
   tarts 44
pumpernickel & tuna 'mille feuille' 63
pumpkin purée with hazelnut macarons 16

R

radishes, pickled vegetable bundles 66
raspberry
   choux craquelin buns 148–9
   Linzer torte 122–3
   & raw cacao scones 74–5
   tartelettes aux fruit 118–91
   triple marble bundt cake 108–9
   & white chocolate domes 132–3
rice pudding, Indian kheer 141
ricotta cheese
   in salmon mousse 31
   spinach & pine nut wholemeal tartlets 47
roast beef, watercress & horseradish brioche buns
   51, 53
rocket 62, 63

rolls
    herby lobster 58–9
    roast beef, watercress & horseradish brioche 51, 53
    tequila king prawn sliders 60–1
Roquefort, pear & walnut tartlets 37
rose
    in kheer 141
    in Persian syllabub 140
    & pistachio financiers 88–9
    & pistachio scones 71, 73
roulade, egg Florentine 54–5

S

saffron crème pâtissière 139
salmon
    & keta tartare, with spinach focaccia 50, 52
    vanilla-cured, on beetroot & caraway bread 56–7
salmon, smoked
    with lemon & pepper macarons 14–15
    mousse with Paris-Brest 30–1
sandwiches
    cacao beef on pain perdu 64–5
    egg Florentine roulade 54–5
    herby lobster rolls 58–9
    paprika chicken ciabattas 62
    roast beef, watercress & horseradish brioche
      buns 51, 53
    spinach focaccia with salmon & keta tartare
      50, 52
    tequila king prawn sliders 60–1
    tuna & pumpernickel 'mille feuille' 63
    vanilla-cured salmon on beetroot & caraway
      bread 56–7
scallops, tartelettes de Saint Jacques 34–5
Scandinavian apple cake 94–5
scones
    Aperol sultana 78–9
    cheese 81
    classic buttermilk 68
    lemon 70, 72
    orange blossom & bee pollen 69

panettone 76–7
pistachio & rose 71, 73
raw cacao & raspberry 74–5
wholemeal 80
shortbread
    lavender hearts 163
    Palets Breton 156–7
shortcrust pastry 36, 47, 118
    spinach
    egg Florentine roulade 54–5
    focaccia with salmon & keta tartare 50, 52
    & pine nut wholemeal tartlets 46–7
strawberries
    ombré cake 112–13
    tartelettes aux fruit 118–91
sugar-free recipes, carrot & coconut cake 86–7
sultanas
    light Italian fruit cake 104
    Scandinavian apple cake 94
    in scones 78–9, 80
Sweet Valentine menu 10
syllabub, Persian 140

T

tahini cookies 170
tarts, savoury
    Camembert & apple, with walnut drizzle 44–5
    curried crab 38, 40
    pear, Roquefort & walnut tartlets 37
    spinach & pine nut wholemeal tartlets 46–7
    tartelettes de Saint Jacques 34–5
    tartes flambées 38–9, 41
    tomato, olive & mozzarella 42–3
tarts, sweet
    chocolate & ginger 115, 117
    French blueberry 120–1
    Linzer torte 122–3
    tartelettes aux fruit 118–19
tea
    loaf, orange & cranberry 93
    making perfect cup 9

matcha & lemon cake 116
matching to food 8
tomato
    caprice profiteroles 29
    olive & mozzarella tarts 42–3
    paprika chicken ciabattas 62
tuna & pumpernickel 'mille feuille' 63

V

Valentine menu 10
vanilla
    in biscuits 154, 159, 167, 170
    cacao beef on pain perdu 65
    in cake 86, 90, 97, 103, 108, 112, 128
    in crème pâtissière/custard 118, 139, 145
    flavoured black tea 10
    in tarts 117, 118, 122
    vanilla-cured salmon 56
    wholemeal scones 80
vegetable bundles, slightly pickled 66
Viennese butter biscuits 154–5

W

walnuts
    & banana bundt cake 84–5
    & coffee cake 100–1
    & dolcelatte macarons 17
    drizzle, with Camembert & apple tarts 44
    pear & Roquefort tartlets 37
    Scandinavian apple cake 94
water, for making tea 9
watercress 53
white tea 8
wholemeal
    scones 80
    shortcrust pastry 47
whoopie pies, cranberry & white chocolate 150–1

Author's acknowledgements

I would like to thank Denise Bates and the dynamic team at Mitchell Beazley for their continuous support, and my publisher, Alison Starling, for putting together the fabulous team behind this gorgeous book and for following its production with such scrutiny. It takes a lot of time and effort to put together a book like this, and this can't happen without a great supporting team:

Juliette Norsworthy has art-directed my past four books and once again has done an incredible job to keep the book looking so fresh and on-trend – her talent, combined with the beautiful stylish props chosen by Liz Belton, really bring together the glamour of an afternoon tea.

This book has really come alive with the gorgeous photography by Kate Whitaker, who has surpassed herself, and who made the photoshoot so much fun for us all. Kate – thank you for coming out of exile in Cornwall for me!

A new addition to our A-team is the fabulous Lizzie Kamenetzky whom I have known for many years – she did a fantastic job testing all the recipes and being my gorgeous baking partner on the photoshoot. Lizzie – thank you for putting up with my terrible Franglais and for making extra lobster rolls on the last day so we could celebrate the book in style with vintage champagne!

Another important person who has worked on my previous books is managing editor Sybella Stephens who, as well as putting the book together and editing my recipes, kept everyone working together smoothly even when under pressure.

I would like to give a big *merci* to Team Eric for their support and hard work: Jean my publicist, Frances at Mitchell Beazley, Liz at Hachette US, and, of course, my fantastic team at Cake Boy.

Finally, a big thank you and extra petting to Bobby cat for putting up with all our antics during the photoshoot… we all love you.

Eric x